To my cousin
F. Louise Schmid
from
Mrs F Weaver

J. G. Woerner.

J. GABRIEL WOERNER

A
BIOGRAPHICAL
SKETCH

By
WILLIAM F. WOERNER

ST. LOUIS, MO.
1912

Copyright, 1912,
By
WM. F. WOERNER.

*Press of
Nixon-Jones Printing Co.,
St. Louis, Mo.*

To my beloved children, denied the priceless boon of knowing in the life their lovable grandfather, whose honored name is borne in full by my elder son, this sketch is affectionately dedicated, in the hope that it may in some measure, however slight, shed further light upon that noble life which my dearest wish would have them emulate.

Foreword	5
Early Life	7
In the Ozarks	13
At the Press—Budding Manhood	21
A Trip Abroad and a Side Trip	26
Courtship and Marriage	33
At the Bar	36
Early Political Life	41
Campaigns for Judge of Probate	53
On the Bench	64
Legal Works	71
Early Literary Efforts	77
Later Literary Works—"Die Sclavin"	88
"The Rebel's Daughter"	97
Recreations	106
Characteristics	110
Homes	118
The Man	122
Thy Life (Verse)	129

FOREWORD.

NO man with a proper realization of his task should presume to attempt as much as a short sketch of the life of J. Gabriel Woerner without feeling a sense of due reverence in his heart, and a full consciousness that though he bring to bear the sincerest faithfulness in his effort, he must yet of necessity fall far short of doing justice to his subject.

For here was a man universal. The wide activities of his busy life were in perfect adjustment at every angle and point of contact with his diversified environments in all their broad sweep.

It is the tendency of human nature that men great and successful in some particular direction become over-balanced; that is, by dwelling too much within the sphere of the particular specialty in which they excel, they come to overrate its significance, and lose the proper sense of proportion and relation to those other affairs which go to make life whole. This is especially true of what we call "self-made men."

Not so with Gabriel Woerner. Though possessing demonstrated greatness of the highest quality in several specialized directions, and exhibiting marked ability in general in the numerous activities toward which he directed his faculties, yet the broadness of his mind, reinforced by the simplicity and measureless charity of his nature, made it impossible for the little, the narrow or the partial to find for a moment a resting place in him.

Endowed with tireless energy, indomitable will power, God-given ability and Christ-like charity, he lived a life, at the close of which it was well said that "God might look down upon this man, and be proud of His own handiwork."

In here attempting to preserve for his descendants as much of the story of his life as my opportunities, limited by my ability, permit, my main solicitude has been for accuracy. I have aimed to remain strictly within the scope of actual fact; in other words, to depict only truth. In doing this, when not within my own personal knowledge, I have drawn from such sources only as to me seemed authentic and reliable.

Yet, when we dwell upon a beautiful and universal life such as he led, it sadly impresses one as akin to dismemberment and mutilation to chop it up by proceeding to the necessary recitation of cold dates, places, specific events. For these at best provide but an inadequate and unsatisfying skeleton, without the flesh and blood, the warmth and coloring, the life and soul, of the reality.

FRÄNKISCHES ADELICHES WAPPEN

EARLY LIFE.

J. GABRIEL WOERNER was an American of the highest type, in all respects save that of foreign birth. He was born in Möhringen, a village in Würtemburg, Germany, on April 28, 1826, the youngest of fourteen children, ten of whom attained maturity. His first name, John, was not used except by way of initial.

Both of his parents, though then poor, came of well-born lineage. There is a well-authenticated coat of arms of "Die Wörner," but his democratic instinct made him rather indifferent to it. What may be the meaning or significance of the strange figures and checkered field, the lapse of time has veiled in mystery.

As a boy of seven he came with his parents and some of the children to this country. They followed some of the others who had already preceded them, leaving only Christian, the eldest, in the Fatherland. The family tarried for four years in Philadelphia, where little Gabriel was put to work carrying bread before daylight for a brother-in-law much older than himself who conducted a bakery business.

Though we have much earlier letters, the one in which the earliest incident in his life to which reference is made, is one written by him to Mrs. Kate Ball (nee Weinert), a part of which runs thus: "I distinctly recollect some incidents, trivial and unimportant, but indicative of the estimation in which, even at that time, I held her [Mrs. Ball's mother]. When about eight or nine years of age I was in the habit of carrying bread, from my brother-in-law Schoenthaler, who was a baker, to your father's house. It was a long way from Ninth and Batonwood [?] street, where we then lived; and as I had also to carry bread as far as Broad and Market street, I was sometimes late, and your father, perhaps, had to get bread elsewhere for breakfast, and reprimanded me pretty roughly for my tardiness. On one of these occasions your mother interceded for me, and suggested to your father that it was rather a hard task for me, at my age, to carry a heavy bread basket so great a distance. I shall ever remember the impression that her kindness made upon me. I loved her for it, and blessed her, in my secret heart, many a time, although I never said a word even to thank her," etc. In another letter to the same lady, is the statement that he was raised by his sister Regine, then Mrs. Schoenthaler (later Mrs. Vogel), and that he "stayed with her from my seventh to my fourteenth year. With Rosine [Mrs. Schilling] I stayed six or seven years; my home was there when I went to Europe, and until I got married."

In 1837 the family came to St. Louis and settled here. His father, Christian Woerner, a contractor or architect by occupation, died in the later forties. The beloved mother, whose maiden name was Elizabeth Ulmer, died a very few years after her husband, in the year 1849. She was an estimable character who (to judge from the vague hint or two on this subject that has filtered down to me) probably had more real sympathetic appreciation for her youngest son Gabriel's character and of its promise, than had any other person at the time.

There is a passage in "The Rebel's Daughter" wherein Victor Waldhorst, the principal character of the novel, in a few simple, pathetic sentences, relates a family experience which (making allowances for variations for adaptation to a work of fiction) is possibly somewhat like the author's recollection of his own family's experience while he was still a child, and which not impossibly might account for the removal to St. Louis. The passage runs thus:

> Victor "informed his attentive listeners that he had come to this country with his parents when he was quite a young boy; that his father invested the greater part of his means in the purchase of a house and lot, for which he paid cash, and did quite well for a while 'until one day a stranger called at the house and told father that the house and lot belonged to him, demanding payment for it. Father showed him the deed, but the stranger laughed at it, saying it was signed by his son, who had the same name as he, but that the house did not belong to the son, but to himself. At this father got angry and told the man to leave the house. After that he came back one day with an-

other man, who said he was a sheriff, and left a paper with father; and three or four months after that this sheriff drove us out of the house, put our furniture in the street, and we had to rent a house to live in. We were then quite poor, for father had not much money left after paying for the house he had bought.' . . . 'My father,' Victor continued, 'was very much grieved over our loss. His business did not prosper after that, and we had sad times. Then came the cholera, both parents took it and died the same week.' . . . 'And then,' he went on, 'when our parents had been buried, and the sale of our household goods had produced hardly enough to pay the doctor and undertaker, we had nothing. I hired out as a journeyman baker . . . and my sister found a home in the family of a distant relative of ours, back in the city.' " (Rebel's Daughter, pp. 28-29.)

Little Gabriel had the benefit of but the scantiest school education; and what little he had was of a kind hardly worthy the name. One feature that I have myself heard him comment upon was the fact that there was but one teacher to the four hundred children, and also that the inevitable corporal infliction that came as surely as the night follows the day was for some time supposed by him to be, not chastisement for misbehavior, but rather a part of the regular daily discipline. This period was probably during the stay in Philadelphia (between 1833 and 1837; that is, while he was between seven and eleven, though the time is not indicated in the passage on this point found in "Rebel's Daughter," p. 27). In a sketch in "The Commonwealth of Missouri" (Barns, 1877), it appears that "he lived in Philadelphia four years, where the subject of this sketch for three years attended the public school, there conducted on the 'Lancaster System' (*four hundred pupils under the care and tutorship of one teacher*) and spent one year at a parochial school. The family in 1837 removed to St. Louis, where young Woerner for about two years attended a private German school, with frequent interruptions by work at home." For this "Lancaster System," see a passage in the "Rebel's Daughter" on page 27, where the author, through the lips of Victor, evidently gives his own recollections. During his Philadelphia period (from seven to eleven years of age) the poor little fellow's schooling, even such as it was, must have been sadly interfered with by his pitiable duties in carrying bread, which required his rising before the dawn to make his rounds.

From an interview in a paper (The "St. Louis Critic," May 2, 1891, which I think is substantially authentic), we find the statement that "the first school he attended here was a private enterprise established by a Mr. Steimes on Main street between Poplar and Spruce streets in the house of one Weinheimer. Steimes lived until about a year ago. A Mr. Mindrup succeeded him. The school was, soon after its establishment, moved to Myrtle, between Third and Fourth streets, where it was taught by Julius Weiser, an intimate friend of William Weibig, founder of the Anzeiger, the first German newspaper published in the city." The purported interview then continued: " 'It was through the influence of Mr. Weiber and Jacob Schmidt, then County Engineer of St. Louis County, that I first had my attention turned to German literature, and under their encouragement I imbibed a strong love for the classics of the German people, and in reading these great works was enabled to understand Germans as I never had done before.' "

But whatever his schooling was, it is safe to say it amounted to little, considered from an educational standpoint, and even that little was very short-lived. This serious drawback of an almost total lack of proper educational care and opportunity, which in itself would have blighted the prospects of the vast majority, he keenly appreciated, boy though he was, and strove to counteract.

With that wonderful earnestness and zeal which remained characteristic of him throughout his life, he seized every spare moment and improved every opportunity to acquire knowledge. By his own efforts, alone, unaided by help from without, he developed the splendid intellect with which nature had endowed him.

IN THE OZARKS

IN 1841 he was sent from St. Louis to Springfield, Missouri.

Between the ages of fifteen and eighteen, as a sort of apprentice, I believe, for Godfrey Schoenthaler (who, however, remained in St. Louis), he was put to work as all-around clerk in country stores, first at Springfield, where he arrived toward the end of 1841 and had charge of the store of Mr. Bruin, or De Bruin, later at Belle Fonte in the same region (from the middle of June, 1842, to the fall of that year) and then at Waynesville. All at that time were small frontier villages in the Ozark Mountains region, in the interior of Missouri (even Springfield had only about 200 inhabitants).

A lover of nature in boyhood, to this period spent in the Ozark backwoods may be traced, perhaps, that aroma of the woods and fields that charmingly asserts itself here and there in the works of fiction written by him in later life. And there, too, he received those first impressions of primitive country politics (very different from the city politics of the present day) which are so realistically portrayed in his story of "Love, Politics and War," published more than fifty years later; and here probably was aroused in him that interest in American political affairs which he ever after exhibited. This surmise is confirmed by the discovery of a letter he wrote, when almost forty, in which, in a reminiscent mood as the result of assorting a mass of old letters, he refers to those early days.

In fact, that peculiar, thoroughly American spirit in its original evolution in the self-reliant primitive settlers, which he here absorbed into his sterling German blood, operated as an invaluable nexus that often enabled him in later years to mediate and harmonize two apparently hostile racial strains amongst the people. He understood the intense and direct German element, with its sincere contempt for forms, even constitutional forms, which seemed to defeat what the German mind conceived as the substance of true American liberty, and with its further contempt for the politer amenities and easy urbanity of the American-born, particularly of the slaveholder. And on the other hand he understood full well from his own experiences, the feeling of contempt that this native element (designated as "Americans") entertained for what they considered crass "Dutch" interlopers, with their gratuitous imported alien notions about American affairs which they could not understand. In the interview before alluded to he is said to have declared of this period of his youth that "there were no German people about Springfield, and being thrown in the society of Americans exclusively, I began the study of American institutions, developing a love for them which has only broadened with the passage of the years."

Many of his clerking experiences in these country stores are amusingly illustrated as those of Victor Waldhorst in the novel above mentioned, especially in the chapter, "A Western Town and Its Rival Stores," and the next one, "Bunkum: Mercantile and Literary."

In fact, all through its earlier pages, the vicissitudes of Victor in the "Brookfield" (Springfield) and "May Meadows" of the novel closely correspond with those of the author himself during these years of interior Missouri life.

By a fortunate preservation of three letters written by him during this time to one of his sisters in St. Louis, we get a glimpse of his surroundings at that time, as well as pointers of his youthful character. They are written (strangely enough when we remember his lack of schooling) in the best grammatical and idiomatic German, in a firm hand, and are dated respectively Springfield, December 13, 1841; Springfield, January 12, 1842, and Waynesville, November 12, 1842, when he was but fifteen and sixteen years of age. Alone in these backwoods villages, remote from family influences, between the lines can be discerned the coloring that this American environment was stamping deeply into the susceptible nature of the youth during this impressionable period.

And as indicative of his eagerness for learning, at a time when other boys would put in their spare time on games and sport, and remembering what fragments of time were his own, look at this significant extract translated from the second Springfield letter, when he was aged fifteen. After referring gratefully to one John H. Miller (who, however, later forfeited his regard, as appears from a later letter from which it seems that Miller plighted troth to this sister and afterwards broke his promise), who evidently had taken a liking to the youth, and who seems to have been possessed of some literary works, no doubt a scarcity in those regions, the letter to the sister (translated) continues:

"You know how fond I am of reading. Well, now, imagine my good fortune in having at the disposal of my own sweet will the best of American literature, the most complete selection of the best poetry—in short, the best that American talent can produce; when I can call mine the finest and most beautiful steel engravings ever made! And all this I owe to the generosity of this lovable man! But enough hereof—you know how much I like him.

"Furthermore, I am most of the time in the store from morning until night, and after supper I either practice music, or write, or read, or make calendars, etc. On the whole, I like it here pretty well."

The same letter contains three of an eleven-stanza original poem written as he says "as usual on such occasions." This was on the Sunday after New Year (his first leisure day, being a few days prior to the date of the letter). The lines are not bad for a mere boy, and are referred to later in connection with his early literary efforts.

A hint of this appreciation of every floating opportunity to acquire a bit of education is also given in "The Rebel's Daughter" on page 26, where Victor (evidently voicing the author's own early sentiments) says of his advent to the frontier region: "One of the reasons why I am very glad to get the situation in Mr. Van Braaken's store [evidently a disguised name for De Bruin's, Gabriel's place of employment in Springfield] is the promise he made me that I shall have leisure to improve myself by private study. . . . I should like to study mathematics and Latin, so that I might become acquainted with the works of great men who explain to the world the nature of things, and justice, and freedom."

From another angle, too, these early letters are both amusing and interesting. In strictest confidence to his favorite sister, and with naive candor and earnestness, he lays bare in the Waynesville letter the depth to which the first dart shot from Cupid's bow has penetrated into his sixteen-year-old heart, and utters the irony of fate that compels him to leave his dear idol while he must on to Waynesville. The name of the maiden was too sacred to commit to paper, and he refers to her only as "S." If we may at this day be pardoned in divulging it, this was Sallie Colley (one year his senior, I believe), who later became the wife of one Christason. In this same Waynesville letter, in order to describe his experience with this perhaps slightly fickle charmer, he describes minutely a social game or dance, and his experiences therein, and it is in substantial identity with the description and experiences of Victor Waldhorst in the "Rebel's Daughter" (in chapter XV, pages 234-237), even down to the heart-aches of his hero Victor in the novel, which correspond to his own on that occasion, as stated in his letter.

More than half a century later, not long before his death, while making a long-contemplated return to the scenes of these boyhood days, he sought her out and saw her once again. But we can imagine what a world there was now between them! And between her and his boyish ideal! Poor Sallie! Having lived the same narrow, stagnant, backwoods life all the time, she has changed little except in years; learning who her visitor is, she now arises from the poor hearth where she is sitting with her aged husband, takes the little short pipe from between her teeth and extends a wrinkled but still vigorous hand to greet her old boy-friend Gabe of over a half century ago, now the author of "The Rebel's Daughter," to which her own life unconsciously contributes. Let it be added that it is probable that, leaving Waynesville in 1842, a new ideal soon developed, the one he had in mind as the "Nellie May" of the novel, but this is in a measure my own surmise.

But young Gabriel must have been somewhat in contract with the Colley family; for, writing to Grover Cleveland on January 28, 1885, the one-time boy beau of Sallie, in recommending to the President-elect for a certain office one George W. Colley "of Pulaski County" (who, I presume, was probably Sallie's brother) says that "it was his [*i. e.*, George W. Colley's] father who, now more than forty years ago, distilled into my mind those principles of democracy which have ever since represented to me the theory of American government; and I am now conscious that the sterling qualities of his character—simplicity of purpose, unswerving devotion to the interests of the public, to which his own and those of his family and neighborhood were ever subordinated, and uncompromising integrity—impressed me, more readily, perhaps, than the intrinsic truth of democratic doctrine, and gave tone and direction to my political views. His son George, I am proud to say, followed in the footsteps of his father, both in forming an unstained character and in his political convictions," etc. From a much earlier letter it appears that one of his close friends in the Springfield days was Lafayette J. Morrow, with whom he corresponded for years thereafter, and whose name is given to a character in one of his works of fiction.

But young Woerner chafed at his restricted opportunities of development in these wilds, "during the best schooling time of his life," as the boy respectfully but somewhat rebelliously intimates in a German letter of November 26, 1842, to Mr. Godfrey Schoenthaler, who appears to have been his employer.

So when Gabriel was eighteen years of age he left this region and returned once more to St. Louis, this time "for good."

It must be remembered that in those days even St. Louis was but little more than a small Western village.

AT THE PRESS—BUDDING MANHOOD.

HE never seemed to care to enter upon a mercantile career. His ambition at this time was to become a printer, although ultimately he longed to be a lawyer. Accordingly, he embarked for the printer's trade by entering the office of the German "Tribune" in the capacity of a lowly "printer's devil." By rapid stages he rose successively to pressman, foreman, editor and proprietor. This experience in the printing and newspaper business is also largely reflected in the similar career of his Victor of the novel.

However, the record of a few months of this time we have authentically from his own hand in a diary faithfully kept at the time from day to day, beginning April 27, 1847—the day before his twenty-first birthday. The writing, which is in German, is in a firm, characteristic hand; the language and grammar are excellent, and the content, when beyond a chronicle of mere every-day events, often indicates a dignity and maturity of thought beyond his years. From April 27, 1847, he kept up this diary regularly through May and June, when there is a lapse of nearly a month, then a few entries in the latter part of July, and a few more in November. The last entry is on November 17, 1847. From its early entries it appears that his printer's apprenticeship to a Mr. Carmony expired on May 1, 1847, and that he entered upon a new contract on that day, under which he was to receive a stipend of $7.00 per week for printing the newspaper, with a few cents now and then for printing little outside extras. He was required to begin his printing work at two o'clock every morning and to work through a large part of the day.

In this diary he reproaches himself now and then for playing too much a card game called Solo, of which he seemed to be passionately fond at that time, but excuses himself on the ground that he can not resist playing with his loyal friend, Mr. Schepmann, whose amiability and winsomeness he praises extravagantly. Says he (translation of item under date of April 29, 1847): "There isn't so much objection to the playing in itself; but there is as to the time it took place yesterday and today. Ten o'clock is a good enough hour to retire for such as do not have to get up until five o'clock in the morning; but my work requires me to be up at two o'clock, and therefore it is highly injurious to my health when I tarry until midnight at the gaming table," etc. All of his games, as recorded, however, appear to have been confined to friends or relatives, and to have been for insignificant stakes. It also appears from items here and there that for amusement he occasionally played checkers, chess and whist.

On May 2d he chronicles the fiftieth wedding anniversary of his mother, and mentions a present to her of a small sum of money, "as a token of his joy at her long and useful life and of his sincere and hearty wishes for continued health for many years," etc. But strangely he makes no mention whatever of his father. During this period he also keeps a detailed weekly account of his outlays and receipts, both of which were necessarily pitifully meagre, but nevertheless he seems to have kept the balance on the right side.

At this time he had evidently already acquired a great fondness for the theatre, and mentions it as a treat every time he attended (which he usually did in company of Schepmann), sometimes describing the plot with minuteness in his diary and intelligently criticising play and actors, favorably or otherwise as the case might be. On the whole he seems to have been fairly well satisfied with his lot at this time and to have regarded the future optimistically.

In a later entry in this diary (July 19, 1847, after a lapse in its continuity) he proudly chronicles his admission to American citizenship, in the Criminal Court, on July 12th, "after renouncing allegiance to all foreign potentates, particularly the king of Würtemberg," etc. Under date of November 12th he chronicles *inter alia* the fact that the preceding August he had voted for the first time "and for the straight Democratic ticket;" he also mentions the marriage of his dear friend Schepmann.

All through this diary he speaks in burning terms his admiration for the physical and spiritual beauty of a ~~fifteen~~ *five* year old girl—Amanda Schoenthaler. Though he refers to her as a "naive" child, the tender and glowing sentiments that leap like tongues of fire from these passages, leave no doubt of his deep affection for the girl. Strange to say (for there seems to be no real reason for his dread) there runs throughout the November entries an uncanny foreboding that his dark-eyed little friend was not to be long for this world—a presentiment which I am told was later realized by her early death. Under date of May 4th he pasted into his diary a "few lines" in type (probably set up by himself) which he "had already indicted to her the preceding year." They are a New Year's greeting to his Amanda—"An Amanda—zum Neuen Jahre 1847"—displaying characteristic fiery ardor, and a literary talent of no mean order. These verses are set forth later in connection with his early literary efforts.

During his newspaper career one of his pleasantest duties was the criticism of theatrical affairs, involving his attendance at the theatres, and his penchant therefor lingered with him to the end, bearing fruit also in the production of several dramas. He told on himself an amusing incident resulting from his constant reviewing of plays. On one occasion, being familiar with play and players on the boards for the evening, he wrote out a lengthy review thereof, thinking he could do justice to the occasion without going to the trouble of attending the play, and sent in the criticism during the day as copy for the next morning's edition.

But in the afternoon, owing to important news from the Mexican War, an extra was unexpectedly issued, and by oversight the review of the drama was prematurely published therein, so that persons seeing the first performance enjoyed at the same time an excellent review thereof in the extra of the Tribune.

In those days the printing press was operated by the throwing of a heavy lever in a sweeping semi-circular arm motion. To his work at the press during this period I have heard him attribute, at least in large part, the great breadth and depth of chest, which was one of the peculiarities of his physical make-up.

And while touching upon physical features I may in this connection add that in physique he was well built, broad shouldered but not overly tall (about five feet eight inches, possibly a trifle over). His eyes were grayish-blue, and though congenitally crossed, his sight was exceptionally good until his final sickness. His skin was delicate and fair. His hair in younger life was rather darkish, but in his later years turned snowy white, which became well his venerable and kindly appearance. His lips reflected the refinement of his character, and the large, majestically shapen head and cranium was a true external indication of the splendid brain within.

A TRIP ABROAD, AND A SIDE TRIP.

IN the midst of this newspaper period the German Revolution of 1848 broke out. Sympathizing with the revolutionists in their efforts, as he then conceived, for the establishment of liberal government, he went abroad with the intention of participating in that struggle.

In a second little diary, which safely survives the voracious quicksands of time, stands his chronicle of the events and incidents of the outgoing voyage. Begun on the day of his departure from St. Louis, April 17th, 1848 (eleven days before his 22d birthday), the day-book is kept in German up to May 25th, at which time he was in London. Thereafter the chronicler adopted English shorthand. This idea probably resulted from his Philadelphia visit, where he saw his cousin Stiltz learning it, and he resorted to it in the diary, probably to improve himself by practice; but since he was still in the earlier stages of this system, I found it difficult to decipher much thereof. However, the longhand part is in the same firm hand and masterful German diction which was characteristic of him. These entries are brim full of interesting and instructive observations, descriptions and character sketching.

Nor should mention be omitted of a decided dash of romance that developed during his side trip of a few days in Philadelphia, where he visited a number of relatives, and made friendships which he never forgot. It appears that he particularly revelled in the charming society of two beautiful young ladies, namely his "cousins, Kaetchen Weinert and Mary Ann Stiltz" (who afterwards respectively became Mrs. Kate Ball and Mrs. Mary Ann Wagner). Although permitted but a few days to tarry, yet by the time inexorable necessity sternly ordered him on or miss his liner, his heart was filled with gloom at parting from them (and particularly Katie).

Let us digress here a moment to add that he ever cherished all the Philadelphia friends he made on this visit. He not only corresponded with them on this trip abroad, and visited them on his return voyage, but kept up a beautiful and interesting interchange of letters until late in life, particularly with Mary, and her younger sister Maggie, but not so much with Katie. He visited such of them, male and female, as were in that city, in 1865, when he, as one of a number of Councilmen (or possibly as manager of the House of Refuge) on a tour of investigation, passed through, and again in 1866 when there in behalf of information connected with the House of Refuge, and also at other times.

He never tired of inviting them and theirs to his St. Louis home. For instance twenty-three years after his first visit, writing on May 8,

1871, to his cousin (their brother) George Stiltz (who had removed to Indianapolis), we find him saying of these two aforesaid charming cousins (both of course long before married, but still Philadelphians): "On last Saturday week we were most agreeably surprised by the appearance among us of my dearly beloved cousins, Mary Ann Wagner and Kate Ball—amiable and lovely as ever, and as natural as life, only—especially in the case of Mrs. Ball—a little more so. If you remember, how thoroughly I was captivated by these ladies in the days when you studied phonography in your father's shoe-store, and I came among them a raw and rather awkward and bashful youth from the far West, you may imagine, but I certainly cannot describe to you, my joy," etc. It may be added that the visit referred to proved so pleasant to both the visitors and Judge and Mrs. Woerner, that it was lengthened to a stay of several weeks. There are numerous other charming letters that attest the permanency of these early Philadelphia friendships.

Returning now from this digression, this route as described in the diary above referred to, from St. Louis to the Seaboard as made at that day (1848), is in itself of interest, if only by way of contrast with travel at this day. It shows him taking passage on the river steamboat "Taglioni" down the Mississippi, and up the Ohio as far as Pittsburg (arriving April 25th). Thence on the steamer "Baltic" up the Monongahela to Brownsville (arriving the following night), departing at 7 a. m. by stage to Cumberland (arriving at 2 a. m.), thence by rail to Baltimore, arriving that night, April 28th, which was eleven days after leaving St. Louis. He gives an interesting account of a day spent in Washington, of its art works and the session of Congress. From Baltimore he then goes on his memorable visit to Philadelphia, where he tarried until a peremptory telegram forced him on May 5th to leave, sad and gloomy, for New York. He went by rail to Amboy, and finally on the "superb steamboat John Potter" to New York, where that vessel arrived at 12 o'clock. And at 2 p. m. that day, May 6th, 1848, the "Sarah Sands," with young Woerner as one of her passengers, began her voyage across the Atlantic, safely arriving at Liverpool on the 22d of May. How long he tarried in Old England does not appear, though he at least saw Liverpool, London, Dover.

But (though this is no longer in his diary) it developed that when he arrived at the Fatherland he found that his own American ideas and advanced political convictions were not in such accord with the views and purposes of the insurgents as to warrant his taking an active part in the movement.

There is but the faintest indicia from which could be gleaned his personal career during his stay abroad. It seems that he made his living as newspaper correspondent, helped out in part by teaching English. The latter is confirmed by a subsequent letter, written October 20, 1873, wherein, referring to the then recently completed drama "Die Sclavin," the author tells his brother Christian Woerner that in order to obtain an unbiased and correct opinion upon the work from the genuine German standpoint, he had just offered to submit it to his friend Franz Dressel to whom he had given English lessons in Stuttgart in 1848, and who was now temporarily in Switzerland.

A further faint glimpse of this stay in the Old World is given from a letter to his cousin Mary Ann Stiltz, written in March, 1866, wherein he refers to the sorting of old letters which he had kept, and after speaking of the earlier ones, continues: "Then comes my European tour, and a perfect flood of letters of all kinds, from parents, sisters, nieces and other relatives at home; from newly found friends abroad; from politicians, newspaper correspondents, from editors and publishers in various parts of the world; the contents of the letters being as varied as the source whence they proceeded." He then mentions many of his correspondents of that period who had meanwhile passed away, including his mother, a sister, several nephews and nieces, two brothers-in-law, etc., mentions that the years 1848 and 1849 were eventful ones in his life, and admits the ardor, impulse and emotion then surging within him, contrasting it with the calmer disposition of subsequent years (so he said), as hereinafter quoted.

However, while there is this paucity of information covering his stay in Europe, we do know that during these two years, as war correspondent of several newspapers, amongst them the New York "Herald" and the St. Louis German "Tribune" (and "Schnell-Post," I believe), he sent many articles—"Letters from South Germany"—of great value and exceeding interest from the seat of war. And I have heard it said that owing to the vigor of his fearless pen he was for a time placed in imminent danger of sharing the political fate of so many patriots—incarceration.

A German letter to his sister (Mrs. Günther), written from Stuttgart, October 4th, 1849, which has been preserved, reveals his eagerness to return, not because of homesickness (so he says—but somewhat plaintively), but because he found no longer a profitable occupation there to enable him to liquidate what he refers to as financial obligations to those left behind in St. Louis and which he says left him no peace of mind. The letter is pathetic also in its references to family sorrows, among them the death of his beloved mother in St. Louis by the ravages of the cholera epidemic of that year.

At the end of 1849 or beginning of 1850, returning to America, which he now realized to be his real home, he became editor of the "Tribune," and on February 25, 1851, purchased it from Nehemiah R. Cormany for a purported consideration of $1,000. He changed its politics, in accordance with his own convictions, from Whig to Democratic, and made it the staunch and influential supporter of Missouri's great statesman, Thomas H. Benton. His vigorous editorial battles with Henry Börnstein, editor of an opposition sheet, lingered long in the memory of St. Louisans.

In 1852 he sold to a syndicate and severed his connection with this paper.

COURTSHIP AND MARRIAGE.

IN this same year, 1852, after a courtship by no means devoid of romance, and full of loving sentiment, he won from his rivals the gentle heart of Emilie Plass, than which none truer or purer ever beat in woman's breast. On November 16th following, these two joined their lives in that happy union that was only dissolved by the Grim Reaper almost a half-century later. She was a native of Embden in East Friesland, Hanover, near the Holland border. She, too, had come to America as a child with her parents. Her father was Friedrich Plass, native of Hanover ("Gutbesitzer in Westerfeld, bei Aurich, tracing his genealogy to Johann Plass, who came to Verden from Stedebergen in 1610). Her mother was Henrietta, nee Teissen, native of Embden. Emilie was the fifth of eight children.

In the letter of March 11, 1866, above mentioned, to his sedate cousin Mary of Philadelphia (referring to his old correspondence), he says: "During the year succeeding my return, in 1850, I received a large number of letters, and many from Philadelphia. I was full of life, full of ambition, full of hope. These letters [he means this period] form an epoch in my life also, and it is quite natural that I should, at the time, have deemed myself peculiarly favored by fortune, and yet very ill used. I am happy to say that upon my marriage with Emilie, my dear, adored wife, the turbulence of my spirit was quieted, and I gradually settled down into the quiet, matter-of-fact, busy lawyer that I have become." (But let me just here interpolate that he nevertheless never did become "matter-of-fact," and that his blood ran warm and red to the last year of his life.)

Happy were these two—Gabriel and Emilie Woerner—in each other's trusted and steadfast love, a sweet love which was only strengthened by the trials and solicitude resulting from Mrs. Woerner's delicate health, which caused her much illness, but which with characteristic fortitude she bravely bore to the end.

During his courtship the warm love that filled the young swain's heart frequently overflowed in beautiful and tender verse. It is a matter ever to be regretted that, though these were preserved as treasures by Mrs. Woerner for so many years, a short time before her death she concluded to destroy most of them, believing them too sacred to warrant the hazard that these inmost sentiments of a beloved heart might ever by chance be exposed to the cold gaze of strangers. Only two or three most treasured she did not find the heart to destroy. But these tender and beautiful verses she kept for her eyes alone, and I must now hearken to her silent veto to their publication.

Some of the letters daily interchanged during such rare times as his duties called him away from her side, remain, too, pathetically manifesting the close sympathetic accordance between these two, and the loving tenderness and simple devotion of each to the other, as well as their ever watchful parental love and solicitude for us children.

I may say here that, in all, five children came to them. The first-born, Adolph, was soon carried off, in 1854, as a seven-months infant, by cholera. The others still live in St. Louis, namely: Rose G., born December 16, 1859, and now wife of Benjamin W. McIlvaine; Gabrielle, always called Ella, born September 7, 1862, widow of Charles Gildehaus; William F. (myself), born August 20, 1864, husband of Agnes T. Judge; and Alice E., born June 13, 1869, wife of Sylvester C. Judge.

AT THE BAR.

DURING the next two or three years, after his marriage in 1852, and while holding the position of clerkship of the then Recorder's Court (below mentioned), he studied law as best he could in the office of C. C. Simmons. In 1855 he was admitted to the bar, after short questioning as to his eligibility, by Judge Alexander Hamilton. The new aspirant for legal honors was then twenty-nine years old. For a short period practicing alone, he then continued his professional labors for a time as a member of the law firm of Simmons, Woerner and Billings, afterwards Simmons & Woerner. He proved to be splendidly endowed with that valuable quality in a lawyer known in the profession as a "legal mind."

It was easily demonstrated that he soon far outclassed his older associates in the resultant business career of the firm. And many indicia point that quite a large portion of his well-earned share of the profits were sliced off in the way of loans to others,—and especially to Simmons in later years—loans he could at the time ill afford to spare, but appeals for which his generous nature never could deny, and which of course were never redeemed.

At the breaking out of the Rebellion his practice was interrupted by his service in the "Home Guards" or the militia (I believe in Company "I" 8th Infantry E. M. M. later transferred to 7th Regiment E. M. M. in December, 1863). He was rapidly advanced from the ranks, until March, 1864, at which time he was appointed by the Governor as "Lieutenant-Colonel of the 3d Regiment in the Enrolled Militia of the State."

He continued in the service until further necessity therefor passed away.

From 1865 to 1870 he was associated in the practice with Edward C. Kehr under the firm name of Woerner & Kehr.

As a practicing lawyer his genuinely democratic nature, his great zeal and energy, and his fidelity to the interests of his clients, coupled with his native ability in conducting their litigation by honorable means to a successful issue before court or jury (peculiarly at *nisi prius*), gathered about him an extensive and loyal clientage, and placed him almost immediately in the front rank of the prominent lawyers of those days. Owing to the nature of his then acquaintances, and the moderateness of his charges, an immense number of the poorer and middle class population (especially the Germans who then composed a large percentage of the citizens), with corresponding miscellaneous business of the smaller sort, was attracted to his law-office.

Incidents in his professional career, and stories of his peculiar victories in those early times when legitimate individuality of counsel counted for more than in these later days, were in succeeding years reminiscently recounted among the dwindling remnant, now almost wholly gone, of his then contemporaries.

The Supreme Court reports during this period contain many cases in which he appears as counsel. Among the cases which the Missouri Reports, up to the time of his election to the bench in 1870, show him to have participated in on one side or the other, in the Supreme Court, are the following:

Baker *v.* Block *et al.*, 30 Mo. 225.
City of St. Louis *v.* Bird, 31 Mo. 88.
State of Missouri *v.* J. G. Woerner, 33 Mo. 216.
Ruch *v.* Jones, *et al.*, 33 Mo. 393.
State, to use of Young, *v.* Hesselmeyer *et al.*, 34 Mo. 76.
Brolaski *et al. v.* Putnam, 34 Mo. 459.
Wolf, Executrix, *v.* Lauman, 34 Mo. 575.
State of Missouri *v.* Winkelmeier, 35 Mo. 103.
Muensterman *v.* Peters, 35 Mo. 270.
Meyer *v.* North Mo. R. R. Co., 35 Mo. 352.
Hause *v.* Thompson *et al.*, 36 Mo. 450.
City of St. L. to use of Lohrum *v.* Coons, 37 Mo. 44.
Plogstart *v.* Rothenbucher, 37 Mo. 452.
Buchner *v.* Liebig *et al.*, 38 Mo. 188.
Lansing, by next friend G. Woerner, *v.* Lansing, 38 Mo. 295.
State of Missouri *v.* Binder, 38 Mo. 450.
Sigerson *v.* Kahmann, 39 Mo. 206.
Livermore *v.* Blood *et al*, 40 Mo. 48.
Meyer *v.* Pacific Railroad, 40 Mo. 151.
Aiken *v.* Steamboat Fanny Barker, 40 Mo. 257.
Wade *v.* Beldmeir *et al.*, 40 Mo. 486.
Morris *v.* Hammerle, 40 Mo. 489.

Liddy v. The St. Louis Railroad Co., 40 Mo. 506.
Karriger v. Greb, 42 Mo. 44.
State of Missouri v. Daubert, 42 Mo. 239.
State of Missouri v. Daubert, 42 Mo. 242.
Paul v. Hummel, 43 Mo. 119.
Kinner v. Walsh, Garnishee of Held, 44 Mo. 65.
Uhrig v. City of St. Louis *et al.*, 44 Mo. 458.
City of St. Louis v. Weber, 44 Mo. 547.
Meyer v. Pacific Railroad Co., 45 Mo. 137.
City of St. L., to use of Deppelheuer *et al.*, v. Newman *et al.*, 45 Mo. 138.
Gillham v. Kerone, 45 Mo. 487.
Meysenburg, Tr., v. Schlieper *et al.*, 46 Mo. 209.
City of St. Louis v. Grone & Whelan, 46 Mo. 574.
City of St. Louis v. Siegrist, 46 Mo. 593.
State to use of Peppler, Admr., v. Scholl et al., 47 Mo. 84.
Murdock *et al.* v. Ganahl *et al.*, 47 Mo. 135.
City of St. Louis v. Ind. Ins. Co., 47 Mo. 146.
City of St. Louis v. Boatmen's Ins., etc., Co., 47 Mo. 150.
Koenig v. Rohlfing, 47 Mo. 163.
City of St. Louis v. Marine Ins. Co., 47 Mo. 163.
City of St. Louis v. Ins. Co., 47 Mo. 168.
City of St. L. v. Anchor L. Ins. Co., 47 Mo. 176.

But the insistent call to public service permitted him to devote but few years to private practice, and after 1870 he did not have another opportunity to practice law until he retired from the Probate Judgeship in January, 1895. He was then 68 years old. From this time he again entered the practice, for a few years. But owing to the necessity of completing his literary and legal works, and the fact that he was in partnership with the writer, who was desirous of lightening the burden of the senior member's work as much as practicable, the old Judge never got back into the harness as a practicing lawyer with that activity and zest of his pre-judicial period at the bar a quarter of a century theretofore. The death of his dear wife, who was called at the close of the year 1898, carried with it his practical retirement from the law altogether. The few months of active life left to him he devoted to the completion of his novel, in which is reflected so much of his early life.

During the long interval between these two periods at the bar, Judge Woerner was kept continuously on the bench. In fact from 1853 (two years before his admission to the bar) until 1895, in one capacity or another, he was constantly in the public service. Hence the time was indeed limited during which he engaged in the active practice of his profession.

EARLY POLITICAL LIFE.

AS before stated young Woerner's political opinions were no doubt largely influenced by the true American spirit, with its mingled elements of Western and Southern life in the Ozark regions of Missouri, which served as his environment during several of his youthful years, and which helped to give him that thorough understanding of the American character. He appreciated how the German was viewed by the native, and he appreciated how the native was viewed by the German. And he understood the value and mission of the German-American in this country.

He was always interested in public affairs, and even before his admission to the bar his merits for holding public office were recognized, and thereafter he was continually kept in the service of the public, in one capacity or another, by the spontaneous demand of the people, for an almost unbroken period of over forty years!

The most remarkable feature of this political success lies in its being won in spite of the fact that throughout his career he showed always a deep-rooted aversion to the trickery and duplicity so largely prevalent in practical politics; he never profited by such methods, never tolerated them nor temporized therewith. He was at all times frank and fearless in announcing his political views and convictions.

His political career began in 1853 with his appointment to the clerkship of the tribunal then called the Recorder's Court, to which he was re-appointed the following year, 1854.

In 1856 he was chosen Clerk of the Board of Aldermen upon the fifteenth ballot, over three competitors (Degenhardt, J. Mulholland, B. Higdon).

Thereafter he was continued in office through successive elections by the people, sometimes in the face of decisive defeat of the general ticket on which he ran, until the end of the year 1894 when he retired from public life.

In 1857, championed by his erstwhile newspaper enemy Boernstein, he was nominated on the ticket of the "Free Democracy" (on the third ballot, over five competitors) for City Attorney, and then (April 6) elected over James K. Knight and John B. Higdon. In 1858 (April 5) he was re-elected to the same position over Henry N. Dedman by a handsome majority.

He was twice elected as a Councilman of the City Council from the then First Ward (serving 1861-1864). He was elected the first time in the spring of 1861 (when eight of the ten wards went to the opposing ticket), being chosen over Locke by a majority of 726 (see also Scharf, History of St. Louis,

p. 694). He was re-elected in the spring of 1863, when he ran upon the Union-Emancipation or "Claybank" ticket, receiving the practical endorsement of the Democrats. He not only led his ticket within the district, but he defeated his opponent, Roderick E. Rombauer, who ran upon the Radical Republican or "Charcoal" ticket, by the decisive vote of 1,048 to 690 (3 scattering), his majority of 355 out of a total of 1,741 in the ward being truly remarkable in the face of the fact that the head (mayoralty candidate) of the *opposing* (Radical Republican or "Charcoal") ticket carried the same ward at the same time by a clear majority of 94 over the combined vote of the Union-Emancipation (or Claybank) and Democratic candidates.

Woerner presided over the Council in 1862, but declined a renomination.

In 1862 he was chosen to the Missouri Senate, being the only successful candidate from St. Louis of the five upon the Claybank Senatorial ticket; but his seat was contested, and the lawless, hostile and partisan majority unseated him toward the close of the session, probably for no better reason that that one of their own party should be seated. But to the next session, in 1866, Woerner (as a Democrat) was re-elected Senator. This, too, in the face of the fact that in this election nearly the whole of the ticket was defeated in the county at large by an average majority of about 1,500.

In the Senate, although a member of a ridiculously

small post bellum minority so far as his party was concerned (6 out of 34), Woerner towered as an able and fearless leader of the whole body on non-partisan measures affecting the interests of St. Louis and of the State in general, and this was particularly the case in his hold-over (1868) session. During his entire career there he performed a world of valuable detail work, notwithstanding a sorrowful interruption in his senatorial duties when the severe illness of Mrs. Woerner required his constant attendance at her bedside in St. Louis. He succeeded in killing a great deal of vicious legislation when the rabid partisanship was not too strongly in its favor. And in the second half of his term (1868) he, as chairman of a special committee, prepared a report on the Iron Mountain Railroad bill which for many years determined the railroad policy of the State and became of permanent value. He "served on the Judiciary Committee and was the author of many useful public measures" (Scharf, Hist. St. L., p. 695).

The blandishments and temptations emanating from the horde of lobbyists, interested in special bills, big or little, to squeeze milk from the great legislative teat for selfish consumption, made about as much impression on him as drops of water on a fat duck's back.

But he studied the merits of every bill and his actions were guided solely thereby. His alertness, his keen insight, his forceful logic, coupled with his square honesty and winning personal qualities, made him the most powerful factor for the good that there was in that body, especially during his second session. He went back home at the close more respected than ever, standing higher in the esteem of his fellow-members whether politically friend or foe. But he was poorer in dollars, almost embarrassingly so.

His struggle against the unjust reconstruction measures is touched upon later.

Meanwhile, in 1864, he had responded to his party's forlorn call to stand for the city Mayoralty. He was deemed by his party as the man best qualified to keep to the lowest figure a then certain and foregone adverse majority—a compliment fully justified by the result. There was of course no hope of success for the Democracy in those years, and the race was but a voluntary sacrifice to preserve the party organization. Though there remained in that party a body of powerful men known as "War Democrats," to which men of Woerner's class belonged (and to whose loyalty to the Union cause above party, by the way, this country owes its life), yet the extreme radical sentiment then in complete ascendency damned without distinction everybody designated by the name Democrat; besides which such thereof as were Southern sympathizers had not the privilege of voting.

In this year (1864), as he had done in 1860, he voted for Abraham Lincoln for President, as the man most nearly representing his own views.

In 1864-1865 he was appointed and prepared the official revision of the City Ordinances. This well-digested and valuable work was officially printed the next year and is known as The Revised Ordinances of St. Louis, 1866. He received therefor the regular compensation of four thousand dollars, most welcome to him at the time, and which I have heard him allude to as being "the easiest money I ever earned."

From June, 1865, to 1870, he officiated as one of the Board of Managers of the House of Refuge; and in 1872 (although then Probate Judge) he was appointed and for some time served as a member of a board created that year by law, known as the "Board of Guardians." Especially with reference to the House of Refuge did he perform valuable service. It is unnecessary to state that he attended to his duties with the utmost faithfulness, though without compensation. His investigations and reports manifest that care as to detail which were demanded by that high sense of honor and that appreciation of responsibility to every trust, public or private, high or humble, which formed a vital part of his very nature.

The time and labor spent for the institution was, of course, from a pecuniary standpoint unprofitable to him and even expensive; but from his own standpoint he was amply rewarded by the knowledge that his services were of real benefit "to that unfortunate class of human beings that is thrown upon public charity and the guardianship of the State for that training and education which more fortunate children obtain from the love and affection of parents and relatives." And he fully appreciated "the vast field for the exercise of Christian benevolence and philanthropy, not to say of prudent statesmanship, which the condition of the poor children affords, who are isolated from the community in consequence of their own crimes or the criminality or poverty of their parents and guardians." In a letter to a married cousin touching the responsibilities of motherhood, he adds: "For a mother, the duty is comparatively an easy one. The all-powerful instinct of a mother's love for her offspring renders tolerable and even delightful the cares, anxieties, self-sacrifices, which are demanded by the little ones. Mutual affection alone is capable of divining what course it is best to pursue with regard to them; to a stranger this may be very difficult. And yet, a thorough knowledge of the individuality of each child is essential to its proper treatment. No two human beings, even children, are exactly alike. It is to the want of attention to this necessity, that so much of the ill-success in treatment in reformatories is to be ascribed. . . . I have become warmly enlisted in the subject of training the unfortunate little ones who, on account of their own faults or the faults of their natural protectors, have lost the inestimable blessing of home."

In 1868 he declined a proffered nomination for Congress, on the ground that financially he could not afford to accept the position. But he was named as one of the electors-at-large for the State in the Presidential race on the Seymour and Blair ticket. Senator Woerner was in much demand, and made numerous telling speeches to the voters in different parts of the State, both in English and in German, in that campaign.

The years following the bitter struggle for the vindication and preservation of the Union, which had been fought so that "government of the people, by the people and for the people, might not perish from the earth," were sad years of political extremes and grave excesses.

Senator Woerner, who had himself borne arms in the Union cause in the military service, and who had twice supported Abraham Lincoln for the Presidency of the United States, was one of that noble but comparatively small body of sober-minded patriots who kept their heads in this political chaos. They saw that in its bitter reaction against Secession, triumphant and exultant Federalism threatened by its own excesses to undo the very thing it had drenched the country in blood to establish, by practically destroying the lately rebellious States.

These men appreciated deeply that the Union must be preserved against destruction by the States; but they were big enough also to have the deeper insight that the integrity of the Nation conditions not only that the State shall not destroy the Union, but also that the Union shall not destroy the State. Disfranchisement and denial of equal rights to Southern States by the North, or to any State, means the destruction of the Union just as much as the withdrawal of the same States by Secession. The Whole must not be destroyed by any of its parts, nor any of the parts by the Whole.

Senator Woerner was the uncompromising foe of the unjust and oppressive reconstruction measures. It may be here observed that though of course he had at all times been opposed to the institution of slavery, and had always favored its constitutional abolition, yet he voted against and opposed in the State Senate the proposed fifteenth amendment to the United States Constitution, when it came before that body for ratification during one of his terms there, by which amendment it was designed (a design happily without success) by the Radical Republicans of those days to keep in political subjection forever the Southern whites, by conferring the unlimited right of suffrage upon the black population, grossly ignorant and but recently emancipated as slaves of the very men they were now intended to dominate.

But this middle class of temperate and rational men who remained faithful to the real principles at stake in this chaotic period of the Nation's life, and who from both aspects viewed the situation with calmness and sobriety, necessarily included but few, and they got but scant recognition or reward, save by the approval of their own consciences. Denounced on the one hand by the dominant and domineering Radicals as of suspicious loyalty and as allied to the "Copperheads," they were on the other hand supported by the Confederate element only long enough for it to get back into political power (at least in Missouri) whereupon that element showed a similar unappreciative spirit, not so loudly uttered but nearly as unsympathetic at least, especially toward the "Dutch."

In his autobiographical work "A Writer of Books" (p. 306), Denton J. Snider, speaking of the first meeting with his later intimate friends, J. G. Woerner and H. C. Brokmeyer, says: "Both he and Mr. Brockmeyer were strong Union men, had been organizers and officers of the early home guards who held the State firm to the cause, and both voted for Abraham Lincoln that same year (1864). Both, too, were Germans, and I have always thought that if their countrymen, who mostly leaned toward a violent, hot radicalism (European-born, I think), and who were very hostile to Lincoln, could have been brought to listen to their advice, Missouri would not have taken refuge a few years later in what was practically a Confederate control of the State, which lasted a quarter of a century."

Perhaps I may here interpolate that Gabriel Woerner regarded political questions from the same comprehensive standpoint from which he viewed other problems or affairs of life. He hated invasions upon fundamentals or universals under the convenient and deceptive pretext of special advantage to particulars and individuals. In all its insidious forms, he fought legalized theft from the general public storehouse, a theft not the less heinous because the loss is supposed not to be felt by any one in particular, and not the more excusable because enuring to great private advantage. It was fundamentally for this reason that he was a staunch opponent of what is called "Protection of American Industries," but which in fact is nothing more than a perversion of the taxing power so as to throttle trade in the interest of certain favored beneficaries.

Before returning from this chronological digression I may further add that, as might have been expected from one who in his young days was an ardent adherent of Thomas H. Benton, Woerner always stood for sound money. During the famous campaign of 1896 he was sorely tried. On the one hand he could not support a double standard of unequal value which was to serve as a common measure of all values, on the other he could not support the apostle of the protective tariff. He again, as in 1864 and 1868, rose above party, and was one of the few to voice his protest against both by casting his ballot for the Palmer and Buckner independent Democratic ticket.

Returning to our chronological order, in the springs of 1869 and 1870, according to old newspaper clippings, Woerner again stood for the Council from the first ward (in the latter year from the old limits of this ward.) In each case he was opposed by Archibald Douglas, a popular favorite, and although the returns show that Woerner received a far greater vote in the district than those with him on the ticket, yet he could not overcome the proportionately great adverse majorities, losing the former by a majority of 112 out of 742 (while the mayoralty candidate at that election lost the same ward by 420), and the latter by a bare 8 votes out of 1195 (his colleague for the same position and district losing by 284).

After this short interval devoted to the private practice of the law, he was again called to serve the public, now, however, in a different and more congenial field.

CAMPAIGNS FOR JUDGE OF PROBATE.

IN the fall of 1870, much to his own surprise and, since he was a delegate to the convention, also embarrassment, Woerner's name was presented to the convention of the St. Louis City and County Democracy, for Judge of Probate, by Henry C. Brokmeyer. He received the nomination over three other competitors (Eber Peacock, J. B. McClelland, Wilbur Boyle) on the first ballot, the votes of the delegates standing 46 for him to 23 for the field.

In the ensuing election he was pitted against a strong and active opponent, the then incumbent of the office, Joseph P. Vastine, but was elected by a vote of 11,003 against 9296, receiving the largest majority for any candidate on either ticket, the party vote in general being so close that each party elected a portion of its candidates.

His election to this office proved to be the pivotal event in his life.

Undoubtedly diverting the direction of his activities from a career which would have been more splendidly conspicuous in the general public eye, it determined that his sphere of usefulness should lie in the judicial field. With that characteristic conscientiousness which was his nature, and which he could not help applying to any call or demand that circumstances might bring, he responded to the new duties and responsibilities, as he conceived them from his high plane. It would have been the same to whatever mission the vicissitudes of life might have called him. It was his nature to do right for right's own sake, not for ulterior motives.

His services in the capacity of Judge of Probate, however, gave such universal satisfaction to the public that he was kept in this office through six successive elections, covering a period of twenty-four years.

His first term was for six years (1870-1876).

He was first re-elected in 1876, the city of St. Louis then still constituting a part of the county.

The events accompanying his re-nomination were truly remarkable. The tremendous hold Gabriel Woerner had upon the affections of the masses was typified in one of the most unique incidents in the political history of St. Louis—one never paralleled before or since.

The Democratic convention which met on September 25, 1876, dominated by politicians (probably of Confederate sympathies) regularly nominated a complete ticket, and adjourned. The successful candidate for Judge of Probate was A. R. Taylor, then a worthy and aggressive young lawyer, who received the nomination over the incumbent by 60 to 35 votes.

A storm of popular indignation swept over the city and county at the action of the convention on account of some of the candidates named, but chiefly in leaving Judge Woerner off the ticket. The latter was besieged from all sides to make an independent race, but his name had been voted upon in the convention, and he of course emphatically refused to entertain the thought. Meanwhile the Republicans had nominated a strong ticket, naming for this office Leo Rassieur, a strong candidate of whom even the "Republican" (the Democratic organ) said editorially (October 6th) that "perhaps the only Democrat who would stand a fair chance of defeating him for this office is the present incumbent, Judge Woerner." The Democratic party leaders in order to avoid inevitable defeat of their candidates were forced to resort to the necessity of reassembling the convention, demanding the resignation of those nominated, and doing the work all over again. Mr. Taylor, having been regularly chosen and with no charge against him, at first demurred when asked by the leaders to resign, but finally yielded, as all the other candidates had done. Most of the candidates were again chosen, but for Probate Judge the same delegates reversed their votes and Woerner was nominated over Taylor by 73 to 23 on the first ballot, which action "was made unanimous and loudly cheered."

Great was the satisfaction in the rank and file with the final outcome in this respect. In the ensuing campaign Rassieur plead for sympathy by asserting that Judge Woerner had said after the first convention that he would not run, but this was shown to be in reply to the demand that he should run as an independent, a position so manifestly consistent with the Judge's acts as to be self-evident.

The outcome of this campaign was his defeat of Leo Rassieur, who was a popular candidate and left no stone unturned to win, by a vote of 26,564 as against 22,191, Judge Woerner's majority thus being 4373 (figures of Globe-Democrat, November 10, 1876). The significance of this result can be appreciated when it is recalled that in that election Judge Woerner not only led the Democratic ticket upon which he ran, by a remarkably large margin over the next highest candidate, but that the head of his ticket (Sheriff) was defeated by 6194 votes, and most of the other Democratic candidates were also defeated. This difference of 10,567 votes between Sheriff and Probate Judge in a total of 48,755 represents more than one-fifth of the entire vote cast!

Although elected for a second term, the new Constitution of 1875 and the statute of 1877 served to create some doubt whether the duration of the term was for six years, or whether for four with the necessity of a new election for the succeeding two years. Legal complications upon this point were obviated by Judge Woerner consenting to stand for the office at the end of the four years for the succeeding two years, and the successful carrying out of this program. He was therefore elected in 1880 for a two-year term. All subsequent terms were for four years.

The election in 1880 was the first for this office

since the separation of the City and County of St. Louis under the Scheme and Charter.

Judge Woerner's renomination in 1882 was contested by his old rival of the 1876 conventions—Amos R. Taylor—who had much party sympathy because of his forced withdrawal in 1876 after having already received the nomination for this position; another applicant was Louis A. Steber, both of these men being able and popular. But the integrity and faithfulness to duty of Judge Woerner had during his twelve years so endeared him to the people of St. Louis, of all stations and nationalities, that it was felt to be suicidal for the Democratic City Convention not to accede to the universal demand for his retention. The initial result on the first ballot of the delegates was 92 for Woerner, 25 for Steber and 58 for Taylor; but by a number of changes before the vote was announced, the final result of the first ballot stood 102 for Woerner to 74 for Taylor. The Republican party this year was disrupted by a bi-factional fight. After the refusal of Louis Gottschalk to oppose Woerner, in recognition of the incumbent's popularity and fitness (and the futility of opposition), one of these factions at the "Liberty Hall" convention paid him the rare compliment of an actual endorsement, and declined to name any candidate for the place. But Peter E. Bland was nominated for this office on the Labor ticket, and Bland was also placed upon the ticket of the other (or "Filley") wing of the Republican party. At the ensuing election there were many surprising results, owing to the peculiar conditions, and a mixed ticket was elected. For the Probate Judgeship, Woerner was re-elected over Bland by a vote of 27,738 to 6719—a majority of 21,017.

At the next election in 1886 Woerner was again nominated by the Democrats, this time without opposition, the nomination seemingly being treated as a matter of course. After Rudolph Schulenburg refused to oppose Woerner, a strong effort was made in the Republican convention to formally endorse Woerner, but the motion was defeated by the delegates on a vote of 89 to 56. No candidate being named by the convention, the Republican City Committee was authorized to fill this vacancy on the ticket—an authority however which it never exercised, thus effecting a practical, if silent, endorsement that did honor not only to a political opponent, but also to the partisan body who thus, while not openly departing from party regularity, yet did the graceful thing in at least this instance. Alas, such a thing is rare—we seek in vain its duplication anywhere in the political history of the two great parties, at least in St. Louis. But then probably there never before or since has occasion existed as then. The only opposing candidate was E. C. Elliott, upon the Prohibition ticket, who received 284 votes. Judge Woerner received 22,307, and the excess of his vote over that of any other Democrat at this election shows that while his name was not on the Republican ticket, thousands of that party cast their votes for him. Concerning the other offices, as so often in those days, the election so far as the City of St. Louis was concerned, resulted in a mixed ticket being chosen by the voters.

He was elected for the sixth time to the Probate Judgeship in the fall of 1890. He had then been serving for 20 years in that capacity. His Republican opponent was E. P. Johnson. It was a Democratic year and most, though not all, on this ticket were elected with Judge Woerner. The latter received by far the highest majority of any candidate. He led his ticket by a vote of 27,246 for him and 19,036 for his opponent, a majority of 8210 (official figures as per Globe-Democrat, November 14, 1890). His majority would have been greater if large blocks of individual voters had not taken it for granted that his re-election was assured and consequently became neglectfully indifferent in scratching in his favor.

This was his last term on the bench. At the end of this term it was his desire to retire, after a continuous service of twenty-four years.

But the outlook that year (1894) was dark for the Democratic party. Its leaders urged him not to desert the party at such a time. Their appeal was reinforced by non-partisans and good citizens generally, begging him in the public interests once more to make the race. He finally accepted a unanimous nomination. His opponent was Leo Rassieur, whom he had defeated in 1876 for the same office by over 4000 votes.

At the ensuing election nearly the entire Democratic ticket, local, State and general, was decisively defeated. The general conditions were so intensely adverse that, for the first time since reconstruction days, the Republican State ticket was elected, and that party carried the State Legislature, as well as the city. In the avalanche Judge Woerner went down too. Although he ran ahead of the general ticket thousands of votes, his opponent was elected by a margin of 1994 votes, 31,798 to 29,804 (figures Globe-Democrat, November 7, 1894). Woerner's defeat came as an unexpected shock to the people of St. Louis, many of them the very ones who had voted against him.[1]

[1] His election had been considered a foregone conclusion by the general public, for the cumulative proof of his supreme fitness, then at its loftiest point, was universally acknowledged. But this very confidence contributed to his defeat, because it lulled many of the independent Republicans to neglect scratching their ballots in his favor. As a strong partisan, one of the foremost lawyers at the bar, years afterwards publicly confessed: "I regret to say that I was among those who deserted him at that time, and to me it will always be a matter of regret, and I have no doubt there are many others who are in the same state of mind. I think there is one lesson that may be drawn from this experience, and that is that whenever we have a judge who is experienced and thoroughly tried, that we ought never to put him aside for one less thoroughly capable, for mere party considerations. I hope that hereafter we shall not give way to mere party considerations, but in spite of them continue in office an old judge who has done more in his place and who is able to do more in the future than any one else who should attempt to replace him, and let him go down to his grave with the knowledge that he was honored with the confidence

A study of the election figures clearly shows that he still would easily have been elected, had it not been for the fraud perpetrated upon the voters of a semi-secret religio-political party known as the American Protective Association (generally known as "A. P. A."). This was an anti-Catholic organization which cast a large and deciding vote that year. In some unknown way its leaders were induced falsely to place Judge Woerner upon the list of candidates marked by it for defeat, because of alleged susceptibility to Catholic influences and unfair religious prejudices. This was an absurdly unjust charge in his case, being the exact reverse of the truth. The fact was

of his fellow men and continued in the duties of his office during his later years."

One of the unfair methods resorted to was the untruthful charge that, as one of the official board of judges, Woerner had displayed pernicious partisanship in joining with the other Democratic judges, in redistricting the City for the several Justice of the Peace districts in such a way as to "gerrymander" the same in favor of the Democrats. After it was too late to meet it, this charge was loudly and effectively exploited for the purpose of inflaming the partisanship of Republicans and arousing the resentment of citizens upon whom party ties rested lightly. This accusation was the exact reverse of the fact. To such effect were his views independent of all political considerations that he incurred the displeasure of the practical politicians of his own party, and the Globe-Democrat at the time had taunted the Democrats with being unable to use their partisan majority of one because of Woerner's independent stand. He was the only participant absolutely fair. Yet of them all he it was who was successfully attacked before the people a few months later for unfair partisanship.

that while he was opposed to the A. P. A. as un-American because injecting religious matters into political questions (wherein these enthusiasts did the very thing they purported to condemn), yet Judge Woerner was not only wholly free from undue religious influence, but there was no man that ever lived who had in him more genuine toleration and liberality for the religious views of his fellow-beings; never a man freer from prejudices of any sort, or less susceptible to narrow influences of any kind. (See his essay on "Sunday and Sunday Laws" for instance).

The A. P. A. vote reached the acme of its strength that year; it defeated every candidate it opposed on either ticket. And though Judge Woerner received the highest vote of any of those "blacklisted" by it, he too went down.

In his earlier campaigns he might have taken measures to counteract these unfair methods. But the silvery haired and dignified old gentleman was now not only disinclined to this kind of political warfare, but made the mistake of supposing, like nearly all of his active friends, that an open and active public record covering a lifetime was impervious to the assaults of a few base campaign lies shrewdly disseminated for the occasion.

Coming when it did at the close of his active career, this reverse, no doubt, was a grievous disappointment to him, though he never gave any expression thereof. One such as he, who maintains his serene balance through a lifetime of real triumphs and successes in varied activities, easily meets the lesser test of patience in an accidental political reverse.

The direct blow of his defeat did not so much fall upon him as upon those who were thereby deprived of the benefit and help of his judicial activities. When Gabriel Woerner retired from the bench there was an irremediable loss—not so much to him, but to St. Louis, to the public in general—one that can never be restored.

When he retired from the bench and from public life in January, 1895, after more than a generation of active official labors, he did so with a record unimpeachable, unsullied, enjoying the confidence, respect and esteem of the members of all political parties, beloved by the judges and the lawyers, and by the people in general.

ON THE BENCH.

THOUGH Gabriel Woerner led an active life in many directions, to the people of St. Louis he was, and his memory yet is, best known as Judge of the Probate Court. In fact his name is inseparably identified and linked with the Probate Judgeship of St. Louis. This is largely because it was here that the people in general more than elsewhere came into contact with the man, and to some extent came to know him—in so far as official business and their capacity for understanding such a nature as his, permitted them to know him.

For about a quarter of a century he presided there. Before him during that time came a vast heterogenous succession of persons, old and young, rich and poor, some coming seldom, some often, many daily—litigants, witnesses, jurymen, widows, orphans, administrators, executors, guardians, sureties, trust company officials, physicians, undertakers or other persons having claims against estates, notaries, and of course the lawyers and other practitioners representing persons interested in probate matters.

It was the same with all—his simple, natural winsomeness won their good will. His spontaneous kindliness and courtesy endeared him to everybody.

All this was but the utterance of his inborn disposition, not assumed, hence term after term, extending over a generation, brought no tinge of that autocratic bearing so often generated in those long in public office. He was the same always—modest, unassuming, ever ready to help the widow and the orphan, and those having their interests in charge, saving to needy ones many a dollar which would otherwise have been consumed in costs and lawyers' fees.

In fact complaint was sometimes made by a certain class of lawyers that Judge Woerner's gratuitous advice and helpful services in routine probate matters too often deprived them of the opportunity of making good fees out of the Probate Court business. However, the legal talent of this ilk too often themselves were in need of a little guidance, which they did not hesitate to seek and obtain from headquarters. An incident was related, how Judge Woerner had patiently but unsuccessfully labored for a long time to explain to an anxious but dense inquirer (whom he did not happen to know very well) as to what items should and what should not be included in the settlement that Mr. —let us say Smith—, the guardian in question, was required by law to submit to the court; in despair finally the Judge suggested that it would probably prove more satisfactory if he, Mr. Smith, would consult a lawyer to draft this settlement— whereupon, much to the Judge's embarrassment, the meek and hesitating response came: "But, Judge, I am not Smith—I *am* his lawyer!" This incident was not related by Smith's lawyer.

The Probate Judge is constantly called upon to pass upon the accountings of executors, administrators and guardians, which are usually of an *ex parte* nature where the beneficiaries of the estates (heirs, legatees, minors, widows, persons of unsound mind, etc.), are practically not in a position to protect their interests but must trust those administering the estates; tempting opportunity for pluckings are therefore presented which are only too often not sufficiently resisted. Now it was one of Judge Woerner's striking characteristics that throughout his whole incumbency he keenly felt a high moral responsibility in this respect; and he scrutinized closely and with patience every item for which credit was taken in these accountings; every item charged against any estate under his supervision in all the tens of thousands of accounts that came before him, still rests in the archives of the court with his personal check mark on it, showing either its allowance or disallowance.

It was manifested time and again—and doubtless was the fact still more frequently without being manifested at all—that his measureless care and watchfulness prevented the wrecking of estates by the unscrupulousness, and oftener by the ignorance or lack of discretion, on the part of those legally in charge thereof.

The general trust placed in his administration of the affairs of his court was humorously expressed by an old resident of means who said that it gave a man real pleasure to die in St. Louis because he knew that his estate would be so well taken care of by Judge Woerner.

That he was the most learned man in the field of probate law known to this day is a deliberate statement of the plain truth. His value as a judge was not because of that vast and practical experience on the probate bench which was his, nor because of the absolute mastery of the theoretical legal principles involved, which also was his, but because of the welding together of both of these elements by the strength of a master mind which understood how practically to apply the old fundamental truths in the precedents, to changed existing conditions so as to preserve the living spirit without disregard of the necessary letter—how to administer vital human justice, instead of merely theoretical law, to an actual situation.

Nor must it be forgotten that to him and his unselfish efforts the State of Missouri is indebted for many a useful and practical betterment of its laws on the administration of the estates of deceased persons, minors and insane persons, which he secured from the State Legislatures at the expenditure of much time and trouble.

And in some instances he secured legislation very substantially cheapening the costs of administration, thereby deliberately and materially cutting down the fees which were his own compensation. One noticeable case of this sort was the act enabling administration to be dispensed with altogether where it appeared that the assets of the estate were under the amount that went to the widow (or where there was no widow then to minors under sixteen years) as the absolute allowance under the law, in preference even to creditors. In letters to the Judiciary Committee, written February 10, 1872 (when he still had nearly five years in office assured before the end of the term for which he had then been elected), again in a letter to Wm. B. Thompson of January 28, 1875, of the same committee in a later legislature, also to Senator Wm. S. Pope on April 11, 1877, and frequently on many other occasions, and in numerous conferences with the legislators, he showed the uselessness of multiplying expenses and fees under such conditions, and submitted and worked to pass bills he had himself prepared, to obviate this objection. And he finally secured their passage, though indirectly at a loss to himself of thousands of dollars in fees that would otherwise have come to him. These enactments, as well as others which he fathered, have been adopted since then in many of the States of the Union.

To Judge Woerner's ability as a jurist there gradually but steadily arose during this period a grand, unique monument—one of such a peculiar nature that it can be appreciated only by those versed in the law. It was the marvel of his having elevated his court, by force of his own personality as a jurist, from its natural humble plane as a tribunal inferior to even the ordinary court of general jurisdiction, to a position of dignity and authority spontaneously recognized and respected throughout the land by the highest courts and by men of the greatest legal attainments. His judicial opinions and decisions on matters pertaining to probate law came to be quietly accepted as controlling by courts technically far higher in the scale of authority when called upon to review his decisions upon appeal.

His advice or opinion was constantly sought on difficult or knotty questions on probate judicature, not only by those within his own jurisdiction, but by lawyers, brother probate judges, circuit judges and appellate judges throughout the State, and in fact in all parts of the Union.

How a great judge, sitting upon an appellate bench in review of decisions appealed to his tribunal, whose written opinions are preserved for all time in the official reports which are studied by the legal profession as authoritative precedents binding future action, may achieve an enviable reputation as a great jurist, while a rare occurrence, is one that may be readily understood. But for a man to achieve that distinction on the humble probate bench, a court of first instance, whose opinions and decisions are not officially preserved, and which as precedents are of no technical binding force whatever, is truly remarkable.

It demonstrates the universal faith in the deep insight and legal acumen of the mind that could so by its own intense personal force impress itself upon the legal world of his day. It must be recognized as a distinct loss to that greatest of institutions—the law —the function of which it is to secure the rights of mankind, that this luminous mind did not shine from a more commanding and authoritative tribunal.

But be that as it may, certain it is that the name and fame of J. G. Woerner as Judge of Probate has become an enduring tradition in the annals and history of his city and State. His predecessors, his successors—good men, some of them, as probate judges go—have had their day, and gone their way. In the swift march of the years they dwindle to judicial foothills and mounds in the corrective perspective of time; while he towers like a solitary mountain peak whose lofty outlines loom up ever more clearly in the widening distance.

LEGAL WORKS.

BUT while it is true that no law provided for the official preservation of Judge Woerner's decisions and opinions in the particular cases that came before him, yet his long judicial career brought to the field of probate law an enrichment far more permanent and useful.

It enabled him to give to the world one of the few really great law books, "The American Law of Administration." The author modestly says in the preface to the first edition that that "treatise originated in the endeavor to qualify myself for the office of judge of probate, now more than eighteen years ago."

It is the great pioneer work that evolved harmonized order in a vitally important branch of the law which was up to that time given over to a condition of hopeless chaos.

American lawyers and courts largely looked upon probate law and the laws of descent and administration of estates of deceased persons as a patchwork of special statutory provisions arbitrarily marking out the rules to be applied. As illustrative of this general view, on one occasion while at work on this book in the law library at Jefferson City, Judge Woerner, in response to a request from Thomas A. Sherwood, then a Justice of the Supreme Court of Missouri, explained the plan and scope of the contemplated work, whereupon the latter pronounced it impossible of execution, owing to the absence of a common basis upon which to build up a general treatise applicable to all States, with material drawn from a chaotic mass of separate and distinct statutes found in the respective States.

But that common basis, broad and fundamental, was exactly to what Judge Woerner did penetrate and uncover. Upon this solid foundation he built, with enduring patience and consummate ability, until he evolved from chaos and confusion a legal edifice of order, symmetry and grandeur which will forever stand an imperishable monument to his name.

Himself thoroughly imbued with and comprehending the new American spirit at work in moulding the law which he was in actual practice daily administering in his own court, he found the correct conception of its real meaning and its true destiny by tracing the multitudinous and diverse decisions and statutes back through changing conditions and environments to their common law and ecclesiastical derivation from England, in turn derived from their civil and canon law origin, even to the laws of Justinian.

And from the source he scientifically brings

down our probate law through its modifications in the Anglo-Saxon consciousness and then through the earlier and later American spirit, until we see that what appeared confused of meaning and purpose is yet but the natural and logical result of new environments. Understanding the reason of the law in the light of the conditions that gave it life, we can and should intelligently modify or adjust it to living conditions or discard what has become obsolete or injurious. Nor is it too much to say that this work has done much in aid of courts and legislatures to bring harmony, order and reason into the probate law of the United States, especially in the new Western States.

But even the historical tracing of his subject to its source did not satisfy the author from his own viewpoint. He went to the very genesis of that source itself. Beginning with the thought that the realization of the free will of the individual is the essence of all property, he demonstrates that this realized will inheres so long as the thing remains property, and that the death of the owner does not extinguish it. The law of successions is but the continued recognition of this rational will of the deceased owner by the law itself, which supplies the universal or rational will for the deceased owner in the direction of his property in so far as he has not himself expressed his will, or has sought to do so capriciously.

The author sets forth this philosophical thought in the profound but beautifully concise introduction of a few pages. And from this primordial thought-cell there evolves and unfolds in natural and logical growth the entire colossal body of testamentary and probate law prevailing at this day in the United States, covering in every stage and detail the devolution of property from the death of the owner to its complete investiture in the new living recipient.

The marvel is that while conceived in this broad philosophic setting which illumines the entire work, yet the book is carried out in the most intensely practical manner down to the minutest concrete detail for use of the matter-of-fact busy lawyer and court, furnishing the rule, supported by exhaustive precedent, on about every conceivable point in probate and testamentary law. He supplied exactly what was wanted, knowing exactly what was needed.

Twelve or fifteen years Judge Woerner labored patiently on this book, "The American Law of Administration," published at last in 1889 (Little, Brown & Co., Boston), in two large volumes. A second edition was published ten years later (1899), but a short time before his death.[1]

Immediately on the completion of this first work

---

[1] Aside from the general capacity required for this work, my connection therewith enables me to say that the prodigious detail labor demanded of the author for its proper completion is almost beyond conception.

the author entered upon the preparation of another great legal work, complementary of the first, namely "The American Law of Guardianship." This is a one volume work published in 1897 (Little, Brown & Co., Boston). In the Administration book he had treated of the law where the element of free will (i. e., universal or rational will) in property must be supplied by the State because of the owner's death; in the Guardianship he treated of the law where such free will in property must be supplied by the law because of the immaturity, or insanity, of the owner, the basic principle of law therefore being akin, both really included under the term "administration," and the two as supplementary or complementary of each other cover the entire field of probate or will-supplying law.

Though these two are his greatest legal productions, Judge Woerner found time (and how he did is a wonder) during his long period on the probate bench, to contribute occasional articles on legal subjects to law periodicals, including the Southern Law Review, the American Law Review and the Central Law Journal. Some of these were advance fragments of his two great law books and were later published without much change as parts thereof. Others, however, were in the nature of semi-legal literary essays, as for instance his beautifully instructive article on "Sunday and Sunday Laws" published in the American Law Review, Vol. XVIII, pp. 778-800 (September-October issue,

1884). This latter is illustrative of his high plane of thought, the dignified liberality of his views, and the calm beauty of his diction. Characteristic of the author, too, is the accuracy of his half-diffident assertions, the care in his citations and references, the sound logic of his broad-minded views, on a subject which seems to have a tendency in most persons to bring to light only their narrowness and prejudices in one direction or another.

EARLY LITERARY EFFORTS.

WHILE it is true that a number of contributions by Judge Woerner to law periodicals on legal discussions or matters have been inaccessibly buried and lost, this is still more the case with a large number of literary gems, German and English, prose and verse, many of which were never printed. But many of his contributions from time to time brightened the pages of periodicals and newspapers, most of them anonymously. In the main they are lost and gone with the ephemeral publications in which they appeared. I hope in the near future to preserve in printed form most of his accessible literary productions which have been referred to in this sketch, and which were never published, or which appeared only in newspaper form.

Fortunately the more recent and important of his literary and dramatic productions he himself preserved in book form. These latter, though they manifest care as to the form or setting, and though the human element is always there, yet are more valuable for the thought, the meaning, the appeal to the intellect, that characterizes the content; while of his early efforts the fragments that remain reflect rather the world of sentiment, romance and emotion that surged within him.

With practically no schooling, thrown from the beginning on his own resources, with no helping hand to guide his footsteps, with all external conditions against him, it is wonderful to think where his instinctive qualities of heart and mind carried him. In none of his writings, even the earliest, is there the slightest indication of any lack of schooling; considering his style, vocabulary, elegance of diction and other matters of form, it is amazing to think of him as self-taught. He was equally master of German and English.

His strong love of the literary welled up spontaneously from the depths of his nature, like the crystal waters of a great spring.

Take as illustrative the glimpse we have already had of him as a mere lad of 15, from the letter (in strictly correct German) to his sister. Siezing a spare moment from his duties drudging as store clerk in a hamlet of the Ozarks, where he was then buried away from parents, relatives and the world, he writes to his dear sister Dorothea ("Dorle") of his great fortune in having received permission to read the books of one whom he gratefully eulogizes for this great boon!

In the same letter he alludes to Christmas and New Year's celebrations by the folks off in St. Louis in pathetic contrast to conditions in the lonesome village; and adds that when he found a little leisure on the next Sunday he betook himself to verse, "as usual on such occasions," and evolved eleven stanzas "about nothing" of which (so writes the lad of fifteen) "so she may get an idea thereof, he sets out a few lines."

With becoming modesty three stanzas only are incorporated in the letter. As a stray leaf carelessly dropped on the surface far up on the stream of time, and accidentally reappearing nearly seventy years later, and as giving us a glimpse of his inclinations even in those boyhood days, the original lines (the earliest that I have found) are here reproduced:

>Glück auf, glück auf, zum neuen Jahr,
>Heist's heut' wohl bei euch überall;
>Und ich—am ersten Januar
>Soll ich denn schweigen ganz und gar?
>
>Doch halt! Da fällt mir g'rad was ein,
>Ihr möcht't wohl wissen wie's hier geht—
>Wie's könnt wohl am Neujahrstag sein
>Im lieben Springfield, hübsch und klein?
>
>Doch hürtig nun, nur frisch drauf' los
>Gewünscht musz sein auf jeden Fall
>Drum hört Ihr, darum wünsch ich blos
>Ich wäre jetzt vom Wünschen los!

As another illustration of this early bent, and the world of sentiment that even then welled up in his breast, notice another New Year's ballad, five years later. This he addressed to Amanda Schoenthaler, his dark eyed little sweetheart, then 15 years old, concerning whom mention was made in connection with his young days. The flight of these five years shows a marked maturing and deepening in feeling. It marks the span from boyhood to manhood. This second gleam from out the night of the afore-time appears as a leaflet (hardly now decipherable) pasted into his diary under date of May 4, 1847, with the remark that he had indicted the lines to her the preceding year, at which time he must therefore have been twenty. Would not the tender sentiment of these lines do credit to any poet? Not to lose the fragrance in a translation, it is given as written:

AN AMANDA.
Zum neuen Jahre 1847.

Holde Kleine,
Süsse, Reine,
Himmlisch schönes Engel-Kind!
Wo sind Nahmen, Dich zu nennen,
Griffel, die Dich zeichnen können,
Züge, die Dir ähnlich sind?

Mit Entzücken,
Auf Dich blicken,
Liebe Kleine, kann ich wohl;
Kann die Wonne all' empfinden,
Doch—wo soll ich Worte finden,
Wenn ich Dich beschreiben soll?

Schöner prangen
Deine Wangen,
Als des Frühlings Rose lacht;
Locken, weich wie Seide, fallen
Von dem Haupte, und unwallen
Deinen Hals in reicher Pracht.

>   Deine dunkeln
>   Augen funkeln
>   Hehrer, als der Sterne Gluth,
>   Denn in ihrem Glanze mahlet
>   Deine Seele sich, und strahlet
>   Engelrein so mild, und gut.
>
>   Um die lieben
>   Rosenlippen
>   Zieht ein holdes Lächeln sich;
>   Niemand kann dich so erblicken
>   Ohne wonnenvoll Entzücken
>   Und Bewunderung für Dich!
>
>   Ohne Sorgen
>   Floh der Morgen
>   Deines jungen Lebens hin;
>   Schön, wie diese Stunden waren,
>   Mögen auch in künft'gen Jahren
>   Dir des Lebens Freuden blüh'n.

Another echo of early ideas is an article in the "Deutche Tribune" of February 28, 1850, with which sheet young Woerner was connected at that time after his return from the Old World. He was then as much as 24 years old, and unmarried, but this did not deter him (over the initials of "J. G. W.") from giving pronounced views on a problem "the solution of which (says he) has occupied the greatest philosophers of all times," viz: "Wie sollen Kinder erzogen werden?" i. e., "How should children be educated?" Without permitting ourselves to be diverted by certain amusing considerations that might suggest themselves, the article really contains much food for thought, and is largely an original appeal to parents not to neglect the paramount consideration of formation of character in their offspring while looking after the desirable but secondary matter of mere erudition, learning and development of talents. In the same year (the date is confirmed by a reference thereto in a letter to his brother Christian in 1873), according to Scharf's History of St. Louis, "the novel 'Die Sklavin' was first printed as a serial in the German *Tribune,* and afterwards published in book form, meeting with so rapid a sale that the edition was exhausted in two months;" (to the same effect see "Bench & Bar of Missouri Cities," 1884). I have never seen this story. But there is no question that this was quite a different work from the drama of the same name which he wrote subsequently, and which, completed 22 years later and hence belonging to his mature period, is referred to hereinafter. In both, however, the name of the heroine is Amanda— and the inspiration, no doubt, that Amanda whom he carried in his heart.

Somewhere about those years, perhaps earlier (certainly while he was still very young) I understand he gave free reign to the emotional and imaginative strain in him in a story, published at first serially in some newspaper and later, I believe, also in book or pamphlet form, called "Das Freudenhaus." I have never seen this, and the author, with his usual modesty, in his later years stated that he was glad no trace of it was left, as he was not proud of it. But however he may have regarded it from his later plane of thought, it is certain that this story excited at the time the deepest emotional interest in the public who read it. The issues of the serial publication were eagerly looked forward to by the readers, and the subsequent pamphlet or book edition was sold out almost immediately.

The best criterion of his early writing appears in "Der Salon" (as was then called the Sunday edition of the "Anzeiger des Westens"), in the issue of Sunday, December 26, 1858. This is a story, taking up two newspaper pages, entitled "Ein Weinachts Abend in St. Louis" ("A Christmas-eve in St. Louis"). This intensely interesting little story is good in descriptive detail, and wonderfully life-like and accurate in depicting the scenes of the humble life wherein the story moves. It is written in simple yet strangely powerful language. Heartgripping pathos characterizes the tale itself. It is full of the deepest and tenderest sentiment. In these respects, as well as in the general style (though written in another language), it reminds one strongly of Charles Dickens at his very best in some of his short stories. With compelling power young Woerner holds the interest of the reader while sounding the tenderest emotional depths of pity, sympathy and love, as the pathetic little story unfolds to a final happy conclusion. This story is typical of the German Christmas-eve spirit. We find a reference to the story in a letter the author wrote to Maggie Stiltz (a cousin, I believe) on Dec.

10th, 1865, an extract from which may be of interest in this connection, as breathing the German Christmas-eve spirit:

"Dear Maggie, you suggest in your last that winter is at hand, and Christmas fast approaching. It is, to me, a most happy and glorious time; and even now when I am anything but the innocent child, for whose especial benefit this festival is celebrated, when I am close upon that period of life, when even Suabians are, by common consent, allowed to come in for a share of common-sense,[1] I still look forward with fond anticipation to the advent of Christmas. How merrily the bells chime on Christmas Eve! What an atmosphere of a general, universal Holiday-weather is ushered in by them, no matter whether frosty or mild, whether rain or shine, whether snow or hail! A bright nimbus surrounds old and young, the toy shops and stores of all sorts pour forth a perfect river of presents to big and little children, happy faces meet you on all sides, and enjoyment—keen, frolicsome, child-like enjoyment is depicted upon every countenance. Even the ladies who promenade in the dazzling gas-light on Fourth Street, forget to scream at the explosion of fire-crackers in alarming proximity to crinoline; even the stately merchant, who has long forgotten, in his laborious and absorbing occupation of acquiring money, money, money, the enjoyment of life, lingers near the bonfire kindled in the middle of the street by enthusiastic boys. All hail to Christmas, the season of Love, and Forbearance, and Reconciliation.

"And Christmas is so near! But two weeks

---

[1] The point here is lost to those not familiar with a certain Suabian joke, relative to attaining 40.

from to-day. When . . . I read it in your letter, I recollected that several years ago I had written a little story about Christmas. I wonder if, like me, you are fond of Christmas. If you are, you will like that story, and I am going to have it printed and send it to my cousins in Philadelphia for a Christmas present. But if you are not as enthusiastic a lover of the glorious holiday as I am, you will laugh at me for my silliness; for it is a very simple, artless story of a Christmas-eve, designed to acquaint Americans with that pleasant fiction of the Germans, *'Christkindchen.'* I cannot but think that *Christkindchen* is a favorite of yours and that little Harry Wagner and your other little nephews and nieces will come in for a large share of its favors.

"Tomorrow Mrs. Schilling will pay us a visit, and probably remain all night, for the purpose of helping my wife at baking 'Springerle.' This is another German custom, without which, at least to us Suabians, Christmas could not be thought of. In my memory, Christmas is as inseparably connected with a Christmas tree, with 'Springerle' (ask Margaret, your mother, what that means, if you do not already know) and with 'Lebkuchen' as a well fatted turkey, to a down-East Yankee, with Thanksgiving Day."

Though in time hardly within young Woerner's early literary period, perhaps a bit of verse may be interpolated in this connection which grew out of his experiences at the State capital in the early sixties, where Senator Woerner made many warm friends, not all of them statesmen. Among these was the trim and pretty young Pauline (daughter of a well known Cole County citizen by the name of Chris Wagner)—Pauline Wagner—between whom and him, ever after and until her death (and in fact with the entire Wagner family) there existed the warmest friendship and mutual interest. It is she whom he idealizes as the Pauline Waldhorst in "The Rebel's Daughter."

Upon her marriage at Jefferson City to Samuel W. Scovern in 1869, he composed the following lines, which appear in connection with the printed notice, found in my father's scrapbook, and also upon a gilt-printed leaflet preserved by him. They were written by him for the occasion. It will be observed that reading downward the first letter of each line spells the name, "Pauline Scovern:"

LINES
ON
PAULINE'S WEDDING.

Pure as her bridal robe of brightness,
All radiant in her loveliness and grace;
Unsullied as the lily's virgin whiteness,
Love beaming from her sweet, angelic face,
In placid, dove-like innocence and beauty,
Near to the one whose sacred, holy duty
E'er forth 'twill be to shield her from all harm:

So stands she there, a smiling, blushing bride!
Close fold around her thy protecting arm,
O thou, in whose fond vow she does confide!
Vows joyously exchanged! O let them aye
Enjoin on thee, what holy trust—to bless—
Rests now on thee, which thou canst ne'er defy
Nor shirk, save at the cost of happiness!

And in Judge Woerner's own handwriting, written by him for the tenth anniversary of that marriage, hence in 1879, is the following additional gem, which is here interpolated for convenience, although in 1879 it could hardly be classed as among his early literary verses:

TEN YEARS AGO.

The garden's rarest gem I knew:
A lovely rosebud, bathed in dew,
Just peeping from its mossy bed of green;
And from each dew-drop mirrored shone
Transcendent beauty, all its own,
And blushing sweetly, owned itself: Pauline.

Aurora's smile was on its face,
The Zephyrs paused in fond embrace
And Phoebus tarried o'er the lovely scene;
He kissed the bud in rapt'rous bliss;
It blushed the more beneath his kiss,
And opened to a lovely rose: Pauline!

Attracted by her beauty's fame,
A noble stranger boldly came
And homage paid the garden's glorious queen.
Now on his bosom blooms the rose,
And fairer still and sweeter grows,
As fondly he, and proudly, holds Pauline.

Three rosebuds now encircle round
The rose he in the garden found—
No sweeter buds man's eye has even seen;
Protected by his strong, firm hand
And cherished fondly, they expand
In beauty rivaled only by Pauline.

LATER LITERARY WORKS
"DIE SCLAVIN."

HIS youthful literary efforts, as already stated, manifested a disposition to utter the emotional world of sentiment that surged within his breast and bubbled over in his writings. But whether because of maturer years, or family responsibilities, or because of the terrible sobering ordeal of the Civil War which stirred the deepest nature of all real men of those days, or because of the influence of his study in the immediate post-bellum years of the Hegelien philosophy, or perhaps because of all these influences; at all events in his subsequent productions it is the thought or content which constitutes the soul of his writings.

Though always very careful of his language, diction, style, yet these now formed but the outward beautiful or striking garb in which he clothed the truth he sought to illustrate or convey. He appreciated to the full the harmony of form and content, but he never sacrificed substance for appearance, never betrayed the soul for the body. Even his minor literary efforts manifested the same characteristics. For instance, his splendid thought-pregnant address on Mozart and Rossini at the unveiling of the busts of those great tone-poets, at Tower Grove Park on Sunday, July 16, 1882; and his keen, masterful review of his friend Denton J. Snider's book, "A Walk in Hellas," in an elaborate article appearing in the St. Louis "Republican" of Nov. 17, 1881.

Earnest seeker for truth and right by nature, inheriting a broad love of freedom for humanity with his German blood, understanding the American spirit of the slave-holders and original backwoodsmen of the South and West by actual life and contact with them for years during the most impressionable period of life, appreciating the prejudices of North and South toward each other, in short understanding by nature, study and experience the enormity of the awful questions convulsing the Nation, drenching it in blood, and in the solution of which he himself participated— no wonder that these terrible problems, their meaning and solution, play a large part in the subsequent literary productions of a man such as he.

One of the carefully wrought out works dealing with the question of ante-bellum slavery is a drama entitled "Die Sclavin" (but different from the earlier novel of that name). It was first written in German, completed in 1873; later also in English under the title "Amanda, the Slave."

For a number of years Judge Woerner devoted to the preparation of this drama, in German, such time as was not employed in the fulfillment of official duties and paramount demands. It went on the boards for the first time on January 23, 1874, at the "Apollo"—the then German theatre of St. Louis, situated on Fourth Street a little South of Poplar. The house "was crowded from pit to gallery, and representing the most select portion of at least the German play-going public. . . . At the close of the third act a perfect storm of applause broke spontaneously from the audience, and deafening cheers called the author three times before the curtain . . . and at the end of the fourth and fifth acts he was again and again called out amidst the most unbounded applause."

It is safe to say that Judge Woerner was deeply pleased with the reception his splendid drama received from the public. Writing shortly thereafter to George Stiltz, and while still in the flush of success, he says of his recent "dabbling in literature" that "I have perpetrated a drama in five acts: 'Die Sclavin,' which was performed at the Apollo Theater of this city, for the first time on the 23rd ult., to a very crowded house—filled, no doubt, very largely if not entirely by personal friends. This later circumstance contributed in no small degree to lessen my gratification over the very enthusiastic applause with which my piece was received. . . . But the most gratifying proof of the popularity of 'Die Sclavin' is the fact, that it has been played to equally crowded houses ever since—at least until last Tuesday, when I withdrew it to make some necessary alterations; and the applause was equally enthusiastic in every repetition. . . . Of course, there were a great many little incongruities in the performance, and the actors did not quite come up to my idea of how the piece should be played; but I have learned forebearance in the course of my experience, and am grateful for even 'small favors;' and I was particularly fortunate in seeing the character of my heroine placed in the charge of a most talented young actress, whose genius and persevering assiduity in studying enabled her to make herself thoroughly familiar with it. She rendered it gloriously, and I feel that I am deeply indebted to her for the success which the piece has met."

Let me here say that this was Clotilde Koppe, afterwards Stephany. She afterwards frequently played the part both in German and in English. A warm friendship sprang up between her and the author as well as his entire family, and for years she was a frequent guest of the Woerners and spent many an enjoyable time with them.

The play was in fact an immediate success and was thereafter frequently repeated from time to time, always to crowded houses. After the initial run it was reproduced at subsequent periods in the Apollo and in later years in the then People's Theatre, and in the Olympic, both in English and German. It created at the time the greatest enthusiasm among the Germans and German-Americans, who not only were proud of its author but to whose consciousness of the subject-matter it gave true expression. In subsequent years it was reproduced in other of the large American cities. Some years after its first appearance the author transcribed the work into English and as above stated, the drama was played in that language under the title of "Amanda, the Slave." The German version was printed and copyrighted by the author in 1891.

The play was performed on the boards (in addition to the initial performances in January, 1874), so far as I have been able to ascertain, on the following occasions: February 6th, 7th and 8th, 1874, at the Apollo in St. Louis, with Frau Traupel as Amanda; April 10th, 1874, at the same place, Clotilde Koppe as Amanda; January 8th and 10th, 1875, at the Stadt-theater in Cincinnati, Clotilde Koppe as Amanda; November 26th and December 1st, 1875, at the Apollo in St. Louis, Miss Von Vietinghoff as Amanda; March 10th, 1878, at the Olympic in St. Louis, Miss Lindemann as Amanda; February 3rd, 1881, at the Thalia, Pittsburg, Frida Tietz as Amanda; February 2nd, 3rd (and matinee on 3rd), 1883, at the People's Theatre, St. Louis, in English, Clotilde Stephany (formerly Koppe) as Amanda; December 1st, 1889, at Aurora-Turnhalle, Chicago; in the spring of 1890 at the German Theatre in Buffalo; February 18, 1891, by the German Stock Company at Exposition Hall, St. Louis, Johanna Botz as Amanda; October 28th, 1891, at Stadt-theater in Cincinnati, Mrs. Molchin as Amanda. And I have no doubt that the drama was performed at other times and cities which I have been unable to trace.

This drama is entitled to rank as a classic. The

language is strong, lofty, chaste. The poetic lines move smoothly in noble Iambic pentameter, perfect blank verse, and in the climaxes in rhyme as well. The figures of speech are beautiful and strikingly expressive. The setting presents a faithful picture of life in the interior of Missouri before the war. The author himself said that all the characters were modelled from real life and are largely drawn from his own recollections of thirty years theretofore. The characters are true to the reality of the time and place of the play; the scenes and incidents are nowhere overdrawn, extravagancies nowhere apparent.

The plot is conceived with great power. It is developed with admirable skill, foreshadowed in the first act, carried through the grand climax in the third and on to the instructive optimistic conclusion in the fifth. The interest is fettered from the beginning to the end. The tense strain of the great dramatic climaxes is relieved by timely intervals of pure fun, sunny humor, and pictures of the pleasant side of plantation negro life.

Yet to the really competent critic the whole work reveals itself as but the beautiful setting for the central truth which, in such concrete form, this poetic drama teaches. Not in philosophical abstractions, but through the living facts of an interesting story, shines the thought behind and beneath it all.

The drama typifies the inherent contradiction to the fundamental American ideal which was involved in the recognition by the Government in ante-bellum times of the right of the respective States of the Union at will either to maintain or abolish slavery within their borders. This contradiction lies in the disregard of the sacredness of the person, upon which liberty, i. e., the essence of the State itself, rests. The State in recognizing slavery treats man as thing, thereby negating the true conception of itself, which necessitates regarding man as possessing free will, and as inviolable in his person. Therefore, if the wrong done to humanity by slavery is to be depicted in the realm of art, the collision must necessarily be tragic, since in it either the State maintaining this contradiction must go down because of it, or the slave vainly seeking to vindicate his humanness must be crushed beneath the might of the State. The law is the actualized free or rational will of man. The slave has not free will, yet he is man. How can man rationally will that man shall have no will?

This collision in all its broadness is, however, not necessitated here, because the law in question is not directed against humanity in general but only against a particular race—one which owing to many characteristics (mainly that of a lower intellect) was regarded from the then American standpoint as an inferior one, rightly to be subordinated to the white. This American misconception was the natural result of the lack of true freedom on the part of the negro himself, i. e., he preferred life as a slave to freedom to be attained, if necessary, through death; the negro thus failed to attain to humanness in its highest sense

—not being truly a free-man from an artistic or philosophical view. It was this status of the negro that caused the great solecism to become institutionalized in American law, decreeing that man was not man—a contradiction that brought such frightful havoc, not to the slave, but to the master, who thus logically denied and belied himself. "For not till he sees in all men the image of his own freedom, can he be truly free; their limit is in reality his limit; as long as his brother is a slave he cannot be fully emancipated."

It were an unprofitable task to present from the dramatic standpoint the collision between the negro, as victim of the law, and the white race, representing the State; for as yet there has appeared no true hero or champion of African blood in whom art could truly typify this tragic collision. No free-man can be held as slave, and as corollary no slave can be a free-man. Only the Caucasian—in this play Amanda, erroneously supposing herself as legally a slave —can *will* to remain slave, because she herself wills that the law, as the higher right, must be vindicated as against the individual.

The real contradiction of slavery as an institution must therefore be illustrated from the art-view as arising wholly within the *Caucasian* race. And hereby poetic justice also is done, the wrong being shown as avenging itself upon the race that created it. But, presented in this field, the solution of the artistic collision is now no longer necessarily or logically a tragic one. In so far as the enslavement of a Caucasian is itself contrary to law it is a wrong against the State; there must follow therefore a reconciliatory solution, or, more accurately, the elimination of the collision itself. The heorine of the play therefore is a Caucasian, and a slave only as the victim of an intrigue. Laying bare with startling vividness and artistic beauty the fundamental wrong of negro slavery, and losing nothing of the message the drama breathes, the author yet in the end thus avoids an otherwise inevitable tragic outcome.

So far as the dramatic form with its appeal to the popular interest is concerned, this drama received the high compliment of being copied or imitated in later years by professional playwrights in "The White Slave" and other similar plays, but upon a thought-plane that lies much lower than that of the original.

"THE REBEL'S DAUGHTER."

BUT of all the literary writings of J. G. Woerner the most significant and important, for several reasons, is "The Rebel's Daughter," finally completed in the last year of his life, and published in October or November, shortly before his death. (Little, Brown & Co., Boston, 1899.)

This is a novel, but perhaps first conceived to become a play; for, writing of his "Sclavin" to an actor friend (Charles Krone, still living in St. Louis) on March 28, 1881, the author said: "I mean to have it printed and get it out of my mind as a thing of the past—ein überwundener Standpunkt. Another play is haunting my mind; an ideal of a Southern woman, purified and chastened by the fierce war of rebellion and representing the triumph of Truth and Freedom over the negative phases through which American civilization has passed. The collision will, I think, be truer and more artistic than in the 'Sclavin.'" There can be no doubt that he had in mind what in its fruitage became "The Rebel's Daughter." In fact, even while the novel was still hatching, he translated it in temporary dramatic form, for the benefit of a German Stock Company playing in St. Louis that season, which performed it under the name of "Die Rebellin" on March 21st, 1894, Rosa Nordman taking the part of Nellie May. The play was well received, and during the performance Judge Woerner was forced by the applause to appear upon the stage, where he was presented with a magnificent token of the friendship and appreciation of a number of the most prominent of St. Louis' citizens.

This novel as finally evolved is in English. It is written in a refreshing style peculiar to the author. The fascinating romance is couched in charming language; or, as the changing phases of the story require, in diction of pathetic gentleness, or of titanic power.

But it is far more than a story of "Love, Politics and War" as the author call it. True, to the man or woman who likes high-class fiction for its own sake it is entertaining and interesting. But he who looks deeper, traces in and through the incidents and characters of a fascinating story the development and treatment of the greatest problem with which America has ever grappled, and sees therein the delineation by a master mind of the big and little strengths and weaknesses of each respective side, of their lights and shadows, of the final fundamental conflict viewed from the commanding standpoint of Universal History, and of the inevitable decree that speaks the judgment of the World-Spirit of the time.

To him who sees, there is in the characters and stormy careers of Victor Waldhorst and of Nellie

May poetically typified the Great Conflict, and the logical destiny, or rather reconciliation, of the North and the South—yea, even to the final indissoluble Union of these two characters that crowns the outcome.

There is much else of great permanent value in this work, besides its artistic worth and philosophic value. While the author was (perhaps unfortunately) persuaded not directly to localize by designating name or place, there is no mistaking many of the scenes and characters. The first part especially, portrays the life and environment of the author's youthful years in the Ozarks of Missouri. It paints a word picture which brings out with life-like and startling distinctness the delicate lights and shadows of the genuine American spirit of the ante-bellum days and scenes of which it treats. The writer is the complete master of his subject and faithful to his mission. Viewed from the impersonal standpoint of futurity, it is and will increasingly become of great and greater value for the years to come, in preserving with rare fidelity and accuracy a once typical and now fast fading phase marking the spirit and development of American life.

But from the personal standpoint of those interested in his life, to the dwindling remnant of those who knew him in person, and particularly to his own descendants, this work, especially the earlier chapters, is of inestimable interest. The conviction is unavoidable and everywhere corroborated by known facts, that the writer was part and parcel of his subject. Many of the scenes and incidents are the bright reproductions of vivid recollections of his youthful days which lingered with him lovingly to the end.

It is to be remembered, however, that the personal parallel between the author and the Victor of the novel continues only through the first part of the book, or that portion up to the breaking out of the war.

Some of the analogies between the early life of the boy Victor in the novel and that of the man who created him, have already been pointed out when tracing the author's early career. But the parallel through that part of the work runs along much further. One who knows, recognizes in the shy, self-conscious, over-conscientious Victor, in his modest deference to others, in his loyalty and earnest gratitude for recognition of any kind, and above all in his anxious solicitude to do his whole duty at any cost, the same characteristics in the author. One who at all understood him can read between the lines the details of the career of a man devoted to principle and unswerving in his adherence to the right.

And many of the incidents in the life of Victor represent similar experiences in the life of the author, and the general development as depicted in the early chapters of the novel is very like his own. It is seen in the advent to Brookfield (that is, to Springfield) as he related it to the Mays (see *ante*

p. 9); in the clerking at the village stores in which even the name Miller is preserved (see *ante* p. 16); in the backwoods local games as described in the novel (chapter XV, pages 234 to 237), which are a substantial reproduction of the description in young Gabriel's Waynesville letter to his sister of November 12, 1842 (see *ante* pp. 17-18); in the views of the Sunday and Sunday laws ("Gambrinus Under a Cloud," chap. XVI), with which laws the times dealt when the author was practicing law; in the philosophical discussions at the dinner table (as I myself when a boy, sitting at the same table, have heard them from the lips of the Rauhenfels, Taylor and Altrue of the novel, being respectively the Henry C. Brokmeyer, Denton J. Snider and Wm. T. Harris in the life); and so in a hundred other details and incidents.

Nearly all the characters in the book typify or personify actual individuals, who either came closely into the life of the author or who are historical characters of those times. One who knows the men of the days of which the book treats can see, through the veil of the story, in many of its characters, distinguished war-time Missourians, the characterizations in some instances being almost startling in their accuracy. All of the characters are veiled by disguised, but often significant, names.

To the few who knew the characters impersonated there is added by reason thereof a most charming flavor in the perusal of this story. It cannot be fully appreciated without this knowledge. One cannot help regretting that this charm and appreciation must largely be lost to those who are wholly impersonal to the characters represented, although at all events a true characterization of notable persons somehow carries with it a feeling of interest to the general reader, who, though unaware of the reason, gets a vivid impression in such case which is invariably absent when the characters are the artificial creations of an author's mind.

So far as the characters are historic there can be no objection to disclosing their identity, indeed to a well versed reader, no necessity; and so far as these characters are not historic, their identification after this generation would be impossible, with a consequent loss of some of the meaning and interest in the book. So far as I have been able to ascertain, the characters and places typified in the novel correspond to the originals as follows:

> Victor Waldhorst (during the first part of the novel) is the author, in his early life.
>
> Nellie May is the idealization of Frances Campbell, a girl of Springfield, Mo., or the vicinity, a contemporary of the author in his Springfield days, who died at the age of 20 or 21; she was the elder sister of Mrs. Rush Campbell Owen, now of Springfield, Mo., to whom the book is dedicated, and whom the author found still living in 1899.
>
> Leslie May is largely a fictional character, but based on the brother of Frances Campbell.
>
> May Meadows probably idealizes the Campbell home before the war. (See the dedication.)

Brookfield is Springfield, Mo.

Vernal County is Green County, Mo.

Von Braaken is De Bruin.

The Metropolis is St. Louis.

Busch Bluff—the author's homestead from about 1861 to 1880, on Marine Avenue, St. Louis, near the bluffs of the Mississippi River.

Professor Rauhenfels is Lieut.-Gov. Henry C. Brokmeyer of Missouri (now deceased). The literal meaning of "Rauhenfels" in German is significant of Brokmeyer's character.

Pauline Waldhorst is an idealization of Miss Pauline Wagner, later Mrs. Sam Scovern, of Jefferson City (now deceased).

Professor Altrue is Prof. Wm. T. Harris, then of St. Louis, later of Washington, D. C. (now deceased).

Doctor Taylor is Denton J. Snider, of St. Louis. (The German word for tailor is "Schneider"—i. e., Snider.)

General Hart is modelled after Senator Thomas Hart Benton of Missouri; this character is of course intended as slightly anachronistic as Benton died several years before the war.

General Ciper is General Sterling Price (transposition of letters).

Doctor McDonald and McDonald's College respectively correspond to Dr. McDowell, and McDowell's College, formerly at Eighth and Gratiot Streets, St. Louis, both famous in local history.

Battle of Winslo's Run—Wilson's Creek (transposition of letters).

General Seele—General Sigel. (The English word for seal is the German word "Siegel.")

General Lowe—General Lyon. (Lion is in German Löwe.)

Unquestionably many, if not most, of the other characters also represent or are modelled after actual individuals in the author's mind, but they are not within the recognition of the writer hereof, and their identity cannot now be ascertained, by reason of the lapse of time which has carried to the beyond not only the individuals themselves but those who might have given light as to their identity.

The "Rebel's Daughter" was first begun in German just after Judge Woerner had finished his drama "Die Sclavin," but after a few years' work had been devoted thereto the partially written story was re-written and carried on to completion in English. Even before the work was completed, the venerable author was planning its translation into German, but it was destined (except as temporarily dramatized for "Die Rebellin") that he be not spared to the world for that.

The work was completed in the summer of 1899 after a quarter of a century of shaping. Just as this life-story was finally completed, yea even while on his way to make the finishing arrangements for its publication, the grand old man was stricken.

The publication of the book that meant so much to him was expedited as much as possible by the family. They had at least the one consolation of knowing that the readings to him from the printed book (for he could no longer see to read himself) brightened a little the sadness of the twilight days of his beautiful and useful life.

It may not be amiss to add that a warm discussion arose when Winston Churchill's novel, "The Crisis," was published about a year after the "Rebel's Daughter." It grew out of the striking similarity between the two books in many respects, and the assertion was frequently made that "The Crisis," consciously or unconsciously, was largely an imitation of "The Rebel's Daughter." This, however, may be dismissed with the reflection that if it be so, it is a high compliment to the older book and shows that Churchill knew a good thing when he saw it. And his book at least is so different in treatment and method as to exonerate him from the charge of manifest plagiarism

RECREATIONS.

FOR J. G. WOERNER recreation meant a change from one form of activity to another. Idleness, inactivity, was a trial to him hard to bear.

From his youngest days he utilized all his spare time. In this way he succeeded in acquiring for himself a knowledge of the elements of music, he early played the guitar, later became proficient on the flute, tried his skill at composition for the piano. The old diary of his European trip shows him teaching himself shorthand. He became through his own efforts a splendid scholar in the German and English languages, and complete master of both. In addition he dipped into Latin and French, spoke fluently Low-Dutch and certain kindred vernaculars. He knew something about higher mathematics, of the Fine Arts, of Culture in general. During his journalistic period, especially, he made use of his opportunities to amass for himself a vast store of information, not only literary, but of a general nature. In short, in the course of his life he acquired knowledge of a large number of subjects, even those technical and scientific, as well as general and literary.

His favorite recreation, if we omit mention of his own literary productions, of course consisted in reading, over which field he took the widest range.

Throughout his active life he was a reader of literature in general, and was familiar with its best fruit. Not only the heavier, but his broad talent of appreciation enabled him to cull with pleasure and satisfaction the lighter gems of fiction of all kinds. To the end of his years he was never above enjoying a really good novel; rare were those he had not read, of little note the author of whom he did not know something. He was well versed in History, American and general, in the Bible, in the classics, in short in literary culture in general.

Nor should mention be omitted that in middle life he was a keen student of the great German philosopher, Hegel, whose optimistic philosophy (when correctly conceived) accorded so much with Judge Woerner's own views. Among the most prized in his large library was a complete set of Hegel's works, in the original German. Traces of his study thereof (especially of "Philosophie des Rechts") may be seen in his legal works (for instance, the Introduction to his "American Law of Administration" heretofore alluded to), and also in the general trend of his thought. His attention to this system of philosophy was perhaps first directed as a result of his acquaintance with Lieut-Gov. Brokmeyer and Dr. Wm. T. Harris. These two, as well as Dr. Denton J. Snider, and the nature and character of their discussions with each other, are delightfully portrayed in several chapters of "The Rebel's Daughter," being respectively represented therein, as already stated, in the characters of Professor Rauhenfels, Professor Altrue and Doctor Taylor (see for instance the chapter, "Philosophy of Carving," pp. 280-292, and chapter "Philosophers at Tea," pp. 420-430).

But though a profound student of the great philosopher, Gabriel Woerner was never a doctrinaire. A prominent, albeit hopelessly "practical," lawyer in St. Louis once thoughtfully remarked to me that he believed that Judge Woerner was the only man, so far as he knew, whose vision of the realities of life had been left undimmed by the study of philosophy, and who in fact had even been able to make a sound practical application of its abstract doctrines to the actual affairs of life—a concession, considering the man who said it, intended as a high tribute.

But Gabriel Woerner so economized his time that his reading, research in the realms of profound thought, philosophy, study of the classics, authorship of works legal, literary and dramatic, by no means filled the measure of the time left at his disposal after performance of his official and business duties. His energies were boundless.

Of the lighter recreations, in some strange manner he seemed to have learned about every game of cards, or like game, that ever was invented, and was always willing to teach others who desired to learn. How fond he was at 21 of the game of Solo has already been mentioned (see items in his diary of 1847 heretofore referred to in connection with his early life).

In later years he was particularly fond of a good game of whist or skat, especially with those of his own domestic circle. He was both a skillful and enthusiastic player, and everybody liked to play with him.

Even better he loved to play chess, in which he ranked high. This noble game he insisted on teaching me, encouraging the acquisition of a systematic and scientific knowledge of the game. Over a period of many years we two spent many and many a pleasant hour, especially on Sunday mornings in the winter months, mastering its secrets, and engaging in amicable but fierce combat over the checkered field of battle. He also enjoyed what has been described as the "poetry of chess," that is the composition and solution of chess problems, a number of his compositions being published in newspaper chess-columns.

But while he enjoyed all these diversions with a hearty zest, through all his days there was never a time that there was not some serious work to which he was devoting his real energies. It would have been so with him had he lived the length of a hundred lives—this was ingrained in his character, and he simply could not do otherwise.

CHARACTERISTICS.

THE traits, characteristics, the true character of the man, appear from his deeds and activities. His whole life was a mirror of his real self. His truer and more general character must therefore be judged, if judged at all from this inadequate sketch, in the light of all else that is set forth herein, rather than from what is said in this immediate connection, which touches more the minor and personal coloring of his life.

The statement above is accurate, his life was the perfect mirror of his soul. One of his striking characteristics was what, for lack of a better word, I might call his directness. Candid as he was honest, he looked every situation squarely in the eye; obliquity, sophistry, made conscious of itself by the contrast, squirmed and quailed unwillingly.

His directness to get to the marrow and essence was often manifested in private discussion and argument on subjects of interest to him, in which he delighted to participate. He loved an argument not so much for its own sake but rather as a means to get the truth, and to help his fellow-men to get it. A stranger to indirection and evasion, in every phase of life, so in this. He accorded an arguing opponent (often without being merited) the same sincerity of purpose that he possessed himself, and proceeded irresistibly to batter down with sound argument and powerful logic every intrenchment behind which sophistry, subterfuge or speciousness sought refuge, and laid bare with enthusiastic emphasis the fallacy of an unsound proposition.

Socially, the Woerner home was always hospitably open to relatives and friends, whom he liked to entertain, and whose society he enjoyed. But for the formal and empty functions of what is commonly called "society" he cared nothing, and avoided them whenever he could.

He supported worthy organizations and belonged to a few formal clubs, but for the latter had neither the time nor the inclination to attend the meetings. So, although he belonged to the Masonic fraternity and met his obligations, and for a time participated in the work (being the first Worshipful Master of Meridian No. 2, a blue-lodge conducting its work in German) yet he soon drifted away and in later years took no active part whatever.

To all of such things he preferred home and domestic life, and to put in his time in his reading and especially to devote it to his literary and legal works.

Among his characteristics also belong his weaknesses. For he had such, at least measured by the standards of some. But they were in the main the misunderstood modesty of a refined nature, of a tenderness towards his fellow-men, of a disposition to give them the liberal benefit of every doubt.

When only his own interests were involved, he lacked the quality of a pushing self-assertion towards others, so often of value in this busy world of ours where men are in general hastily taken at their own appraisement of themselves. Yet when a matter of principle was at stake, or the vindication of the interests of others, he was aggressive, and firm as adamant. Perhaps it is true that he was generous to a fault, sometimes to persons others would have thought unworthy. It may be he gave too much of his time to such as imposed upon him in that respect, and whom the average man would have avoided or rebuffed. And perhaps he disliked too much to refuse financial aid to persons who really had no substantial claim to ask it. He may have erred in giving when help was not needed. But it is certain, at least, that in no case within his knowledge where help *was* needed, did he fail to respond—nay anticipate—to the measure of his ability.

Then again, many considered him foolishly conscientious in the affairs of life. For instance, he always returned for taxation all the taxable property he owned, though otherwise inaccessible to the tax assessor's knowledge; he was the shining exception to the conventional practice of dodging taxes on intangible property and investments.

Yet is not this spirit of conscientiousness the real, the only, proof of fundamental sincerity and soundness of man's honesty, of his honor? He must do right for its own sake; must respect the general or public call as he does the concrete or individual.

A similar symptom of this phase of his character showed itself when during his long term as Probate Judge he was the initiator and prime mover of much legislation calculated to cheapen the cost of administration of estates, whereby, in the general interest, he lost thousands of dollars in fees that were flowing to him from the very sources he dried up. Wherever he could, he cut down the costs of administration, with an unselfishness that was in no way abated because of the fact that it was not appreciated by the general public, nor even known to those whom it benefited.

He was never what in these days is termed a moneymaker, though, after being fairly launched, he never lacked for money; nor, indeed, was he a money-saver to any great extent. That he was fully conscious of his want of financial shrewdness or cunning, may be surmised from an excerpt from a letter written to his brother Christian in Moehringen in May, 1872 (when 46), although allowance must be made that it was evidently intended (on the theory that "misery loves company") to hearten the brother, who seemed to be in somewhat straightened circumstances; liberally translated it runs thus:

> "I, too, should be content; and if I could manage finances to better advantage, there might be prospects that I might become a well-to-do man.

Unfortunately, however, a friend of mine was right when he maintained that I was entirely guileless concerning all the attributes that money possessed, with the sole exception of appreciating its exchange value. I have noticed that, so far as saving money goes, it makes but little difference whether I make $500 or $10,000 a year—it will always about suffice to satisfy my current necessities, or, if you prefer, demands. Aside from the fact that I have made provision to protect my family from immediate want, I suppose I will die a poor man, however favorable may be my prospects for the next few years. How lucky that at quite such an early age I became convinced that I was not cut out for a merchant, which vocation it had been determined I was to follow! Yet it seems to me, dear brother, that in this respect I do not stand alone in the family, and you especially seem to err in the same direction. At all events so my wife maintains, who holds us two—you and me—to be a couple of incorrigible idealists, far too good-natured ever to acquire riches—do you think she is right?"

But this was hardly because he lacked financial acumen; it was rather the result of his disposition.

It was distasteful to him to scheme and dicker for financial advantage; he was utterly averse to driving a sharp bargain; and he refused to worship at the shrine of Mammon. Hence he never became a rich man; in fact until along towards middle age, he was not even free from debt.

Yet it is equally true that from the first Woerner never failed to earn an honest living, and at all times after he was once fairly started, he lived comfortably and well. He always earned a-plenty to spend money freely in getting whatever was rationally desirable for his family or himself—and that is just what he did with it. In this respect, true to himself, his own personal wants were simple, rational and sound. In all that pertained to the health, education, pleasure and welfare of his family circle he never stopped to reckon the cost in money. Nor did he by any means confine his liberality to his family, nor to these purposes, but it was his disposition in general.

In fact, truly it may be said that with great wisdom in the larger sense, he drew from life its deepest and truest joys and pleasures, and used money as a means to that end.

Keen was his sense of humor. Hearty, infectious, whole-souled his good natured and ready laugh. He particularly enjoyed humor of the more delicate and veiled sort rather than that of the coarse kind.

Of vanity or self-conceit in any direction, he was absolutely destitute. Duplicity found in him its antipode; hypocrisy its antithesis.

Wholly unfeigned and sincere too was his courtliness and chivalry toward the gentler sex, which never left him.

Never more truly than in him did that famous line of Goethe find expression:

"Das ewig weibliche
Zieht uns hinan."

For, is it not in fundamental accord with the eternal fitness of things, and with the deepest chord in the true masculine character, that it appreciate to its fullest the delicate charm and grace of the truly feminine? But it is the indefinable womanly quality, not the intellectual in woman, that attracts as the sweetness of the dew-kissed flower does the bee.

Perhaps on this subject it is not quite a fair criterion, either to the ladies or himself, to take an excerpt from an offhand letter to an informal Westerner, but at all events this is what he said in that way in 1865: After expressing his admiration for a certain class of highly intellectual Boston ladies, whom on some occasion he had leisurely observed as they called for and read works and treatises on the higher branches of human knowledge, he hesitatingly confessed that the pleasure was not wholly unalloyed, and continued:

"I soon noticed that the features of most, if not all, of these ladies, though regular, and in many instances undeniably beautiful, had a hardness, not to say harshness with them, which deprives them of that higher charm of female beauty, that softness, that something, which I cannot give a name for but *femininity*—that which is lovable in woman. It struck me almost as if nature resented the attempt, on the part of woman, to invade the realm peculiarly allotted to men. Combat, act, exertion, physical or mental, is for the man; activity is the masculine principle; while it is woman's province to soothe, to receive, to suffer; passiveness is feminine. And as those females whom necessity or custom compels to live in the field, or perform other heavy physical labor, assume a roughness of exterior not belonging to their sex, so the severity of the mental discipline submitted to by intellectual ladies is shadowed forth in their features, and makes them unfeminine. I feel that I might admire such a woman, be charmed by her wit and the brilliancy of her reasoning power; but I feel that I never could love one—no blue-stocking for me!"

A kindred trait was his fondness for little children, and especially if bright or pretty. He was always zestfully ready to amuse and be amused by the youngsters. Particularly fortunate in this respect was his first grandchild, Gabrielle McIlvaine (called "Gay," now Mrs. Harris), who was his inseparable companion during her early years. There can be no doubt that her natural brightness and attractive disposition were thus inestimably enriched by influences that could never flow from any mere governess or system of schooling.

HOMES.

WHERE was the exact location of the first home of the newly married Woerners in the fifties, I am unable to say, though I do know it was somewhere in what afterwards became the business part of the city, though in those days the village of St. Louis was hardly more than a fringe along the Mississippi. Judging from his then political career it is safe to say that their residence or residences at that time (or at least within a few years thereafter) were within the limits of what was then the first ward.

But along about 1858 or 1860, induced, I presume, partly by his fondness for nature, but mainly in the hope of improving the health of Mrs. Woerner, he strained his slim finances in the purchase of a piece of real estate (afterwards added to and enlarged) which was subsequently converted into the spacious grounds and cozy home, which he baptized "Rose Cottage" in honor of the oldest girl, Rose, "whose birth was coincident with the erection of its walls."

The pretty little homestead was hidden amongst the oak trees, on what was popularly known as "Kayser's Hill," remote from the business and residence parts of the town. For a short interval, either in the beginning or shortly afterwards, for some reason it was leased out, but the tenant almost at once having broken his lease and vacated, the family gladly took the opportunity to move in again and remained there from that early day until 1880. And there the last three of us children first saw the light.

In those by-gone days, even down to my own earliest recollections, this was a beautiful region in the southern part of St. Louis. There were few houses, and many trees, birds and flowers. The land there was still in an unmarred state of nature, covered by verdure, largely consisting of towering oak trees.

Towards the East there was a steep descent from high bluffs down to the swirling waters of the Mississippi. In the middle of the broad channel of that river was "the Island" (since caused to be joined to the East shore), its head about opposite the Woerner homestead. From the rear of the latter a magnificent view over the Illinois side of the river was spread before the eye, particularly as viewed from the "summer-house," a pretty little wooden structure put up by my father within my own recollection.

The residence itself, facing the opposite direction, was set far back from Marine Avenue, toward which it fronted. On one side were the broad grounds of the "Marine Hospital;" and most of the neighborhood was then forest or prairie. The original frontage on Marine Avenue was enlarged by an adjustment or exchange of another part, by agreement or purchase from the Government, owning the adjoining or Marine Hospital grounds.

The descriptions of "Busch Villa" in "The Rebel's Daughter" are evidently drawn from this home of ours on the Mississippi bluffs and its cozy house and surrounding gardens, and convey a good idea thereof.

Having been born and reared there until fifteen years old, my own earliest and dearest boyhood recollections are inseparably intertwined with "the old place" and its environments.

Though some distance "from town," our place, especially on Sundays, I remember to have been a favorite Mecca for relatives, friends and visitors, who enjoyed the liberal hospitality and table of my parents, which must have occasioned not a little strain on my good mother, who by the way was the best housekeeper and housewife there ever was.

Toward the river and alongside what we called "the lot," upon which stood that dear little "summer-house," was hidden a snug little brick residence, also belonging to the Woerner tract, in which lived one of his sisters, Mrs. Rosina Schilling, or, "Aunt Schilling," as she was universally known (not only to us, but to everybody, related or not). This dear old lady was passionately fond of flowers and their culture. Her garden, famed far and near, contained numberless varieties of beautiful and rare plants and flowers, many of which were preserved in the winter months in hot houses. After her death (which followed not long after that of her husband) this little house was occupied by another of my father's sisters, the dear little widow Dorothea Guenther, and her family—the same to whom the letters heretofore alluded to were written, while he was buried away in the Ozarks in 1841 and 1842.

The beauty of the scenery and the character of the neighborhood were largely changed when it was filled in later by shanties and dairies, with unrefined occupants, and by the dying of the oaks and other trees, and by the opening of enormous stone-quarries along and into the bluffs on the river. In 1880 the family moved away, and the pretty old homestead was later much transformed; we moved temporarily to No. 1322 Chouteau Avenue (then still a fairly good neighborhood, but now greatly degenerated); later, in 1885, to No. 2327 Lafayette Avenue (now converted into flats), and finally in 1891 to the beautiful Compton Heights district where, as the second house in that subdivision, was erected the last residence (3464 Hawthorne Avenue) where the lovable couple lived until the end, only a few years later.

THE MAN.

J. GABRIEL WOERNER,— Oh, the man himself!

At this point the writer confesses failure in his mission. Having been constantly with him from the day of my birth to the time of his death, with all that this implies, I admit high inability to tell to another what I know and feel. Speech is a symbol that appeals first to the mind, never directly the heart.

There are things that must be felt ere we know, which cannot be learned from without. What printed page can give an adequate idea of the subtle fragrance of the rose to one robbed of the sense of smell? What words depict the beauty of a gorgeous sunset to him bereft of sight? What symbol can convey to the deaf the soul-stirring music of the great masters? There are things for the soul, not conveyed through the understanding. One who never loved cannot through lip or pen be made to know love. Each human heart may know it through itself alone. Analysis is merely absurd. No tongue, however eloquent, can teach it; no pen, however keen, substitute the image for the fact. No more can I hope to give to one who never knew him, and never felt his presence, an adequate impression of J. Gabriel Woerner as a living reality, as husband, father, grandfather, friend!

Feeling, will, intellect—that trinity of the human mind that makes man the hyphen between Nature and God, and the evolution of which tends toward the Divine—were all manifested in him in a high degree.

There was an indefinable something within and about him that won those with whom he came into personal contact. Some ascribed this to their own appreciation of his high sense of honor, some to his genial, democratic and kindly disposition, others to admiration of his intellectual power, still others accounted for it as resulting from this or that one of the many other traits of his character.

Perhaps each was partially right, certainly none wholly so. My own judgment is that the explanation lay in the breadth and scope of his character, in the universality of his nature.

Gabriel Woerner was a man universal. His sympathy (using the word in its largest sense) for all humanity was so broad and deep that it extended to all who came into contact with him. He understood the good in each man and communed with him upon that man's own plane, whatever it might be. This is most curiously manifested by the fact, still proven time and again these many years after his death by the unconscious testimony of those who knew him, that Gabriel Woerner made upon each individual whose life he touched the lasting impression that he had understood and appreciated that particular person more truly than had any one else. And this by people possessed of the most opposite temperaments and tendencies, and living in most widely different stations in life, or extremes of education and ignorance.

To those in mental distress and trouble his mere presence, the fact that he knew about it, exerted a feeling of soothing restfulness or consolation. Often, without assuming the implied superiority always lurking in direct advice, his subtle guidance and influence helped those in need, without their conscious knowledge, and by methods unseen. He was ever ready and quick to respond where help or kindly offices were needed. His words, his smile, his letters, his acts, were a world of comfort to the disconsolate and stricken.

His sensitive nature abhorred ostentation. His charity was of that chaste kind that does good by stealth—and so he did to an extent far greater, and in ways more numerous, than were ever known. To him the value of a good deed lay in the thing itself, not in any return to the doer. Nor in its publicity, from which he shrank.

There was in this man a rare combination of qualities. On the one hand a powerful intellect, indomitable vigor, tireless energy, a stern adherence to principle, a true nobility of mind; and on the other hand a modesty, kindly sympathy, geniality and real gentleness;—a combination that is but seldom found in one and the same person.

Genial, appreciative, diversified and interesting, original, clean and unperverted in thought, enthusiastic but equable, never proud or vain because of success, nor pessimistic because of reverses, association with him was to all a delight and a profit.

And so this grand character lived his life. In the beginning conditions were against him, but this served only to strengthen the sterling qualities by which he conquered his way, and to broaden and liberalize his views. He rounded out a beautiful and full life, and tasted those of life's sweets that are to a noble mind worth while.

On December 28, 1898, there came the unexpected, sudden blow that bereft him of the beloved life partner with whom he had lived over forty-six years of happy conjugal life. When the cruel scythe of the Grim Reaper with swift and ruthless stroke cut down that sweetest of flowers, his keen blade at the same instant gashed the wound into the survivor's heart which never ceased to bleed. It was the one blow from which he could never rally, and he soon followed to the same bourne, once more to join her, hardly a year later.

After Mrs. Woerner's death he took but little interest in things. But after awhile he did concentrate his efforts to complete his novel, the work in which, as repeatedly stated, he largely lived over again his younger days, and in which he gave expression to much of what transpired during his times.

With that work finally completed he was on his way, in the late summer of 1899, to make the final arrangements with his publisher at Boston, intending to remain in the vicinity at a summer resort to supervise the printing thereof, accompanied at the time by his daughter Ella and her husband, when he was unexpectedly stricken on the train by a paralytic stroke or in the nature thereof. Even then, with pathetic insistence and prophetic foreboding, he would not forego seeing his publisher in Boston, before being taken to Rye Beach, where I soon hurried to join him.

He never recovered. After some weeks at Rye he was brought back to the old homestead on Hawthorne Avenue and gradually sank until January 20, 1900, when his Christ-like spirit was released from the body and returned to the Maker in whose image it was created.

The most crushing effect of this blow—in fact, the double loss in a year of those held most dear—of course fell upon us, his children and descendants. They were ours as we were theirs. It is befitting to be silent where words can but serve to cheapen.

But to all who knew him, and to many who knew only of him, the passing of the lovable man brought sorrow, heartfelt, genuine, universal. Equally so to homes of luxury or culture and to those of lowliness and humility, for his life belonged to no class, but to humanity. His brethren of the bar, in a great gathering of the Bar Association, held a few days after his death, paid to his memory one of the most impressive and beautiful tributes ever offered in the annals of that body.

Until the last is called, will he live also in the sweet and grateful memory of those who knew him; after that will he live in the influences that flow from his life, and in the works which are his perpetual monument.

Yes—imperishable and real is this monument to earthly duty well performed. No one there ever was who not only tried to do, but who also more truly did, his whole duty. Yet as a last tribute to the high plane of thought and character in which he lived, there was inscribed upon his tomb in beautiful Bellefontaine this modest epitaph, for it was the only one to which his assent could be secured:

"He tried to do his duty."

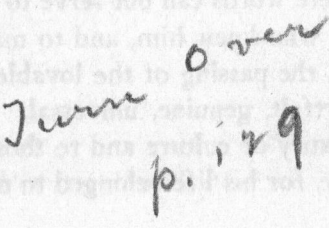

THY LIFE.

O noble life! Methinks 'tmust be
When God from clay thy soul set free,
He smiled with pride that even He
Could fashion such a man as thee.

Thy lesson's soul-compelling might
E'er shines as Pole-star in the night,
To point with clear and steady light
The path to Duty and the Right.

Ancestral star! O guiding gleam!
So pure, so Christ-like and serene,
To thy descendants dost thou seem
Like Star of Bethlehem—God's beam.

W. F. W.
St. Louis, Dec. 24th, 1912.